Special Happenings

Special Happenings

Bernard J. Weiss
Reading and Linguistics

Eldonna L. Evertts
Language Arts

Loreli Olson Steuer
Reading and Linguistics

Janet Sprout
Educational Consultant

Lyman C. Hunt
General Editor — Satellite Books

Level 12

HOLT, RINEHART AND WINSTON, PUBLISHERS
New York • Toronto • London • Sydney

ISBN: 0-03-047851-0
01234   071   9876543

Acknowledgments:

Grateful acknowledgment is given to the following authors and publishers:

Abingdon Press, for "The Wind Came Running," from *I Rode the Black Horse Far Away* by Ivy O. Eastwick. Copyright © 1960 by Abingdon Press. Used by permission.

Addison-Wesley Publishing Company, for "Kiya the Gull," adapted from *Kiya the Gull* by Fen H. Lasell. Copyright © 1969 by Fen H. Lasell. An Addisonian Press Book. Used by permission.

Atheneum Publishers, Inc., and Brandt and Brandt, for "The Bat," from *Cats and Bats and Things with Wings* by Conrad Aiken. Copyright © 1965 by Conrad Aiken. Used by permission.

Atheneum Publishers, Inc., and Angus & Robertson, for "The Royal Tailor," from *The Ombley-Gombley* by Peter Wesley-Smith and David Fielding. Copyright © 1969 by Peter Wesley-Smith and David Fielding. Used by permission.

Childrens Press, Regensteiner Publishing Enterprises, Inc., and Annette Betz, for "If I Were," by Lene Hille-Brandts, adapted by Elizabeth Duckworth from *Wenn Ich Ein Kleiner Daumling War* by Lene Hille-Brandts. Copyright © 1966 by Annette Betz. Used by permission.

Thomas Y. Crowell Company, Inc., for "Footprints," from *Feathered Ones and Furry* by Aileen Fisher. Copyright © 1971 by Aileen Fisher. Used by permission.

The John Day Company, Inc., for "Let Me Tell You About My Dad," adapted from *Let Me Tell You About My Dad* by Phillip Viereck. Copyright © 1971 by Phillip and Ellen Viereck. Used by permission.

Farrar, Straus & Giroux, Inc., for "Mitzi and the President," from *Tell Me a Mitzi* by Lore Segal. Copyright © 1970 by Lore Segal. Used by permission.

Follett Publishing Company, division of Follett Corporation, for "When Something Happy Happens," from *That Was Summer* by Marci Ridlon. Copyright © 1969 by Marci Ridlon. For, "Bridges," from *Day Is Dancing and Other Poems* by Rowena Bennett. Copyright 1948, renewed © 1968 by Rowena Bennett. Used by permission.

Garrard Publishing Co., Champaign, Illinois, for "Nellie Bly: Reporter for *The World*," adapted from *Nellie Bly: Reporter for The World*

by Charles Graves. Copyright © 1971 by Charles Graves. Used by permission.

Grosset & Dunlap, Inc., for "Voices," from *At the Top of My Voice and Other Poems* by Felice Holman. A W.W. Norton book published by Grosset & Dunlap, Inc. Used by permission.

Harper & Row, Publishers, Inc., and McIntosh and Otis, for "The Birthday," adapted from *Delilah* by Carole Hart. Illustrated by Ed Frascino. Text copyright © 1973 by Carole Hart. Illustrations copyright © 1973 by Ed Frascino. Used by permission.

Harper & Row, Publishers, Inc., for "How to be a Nature Detective," slightly adapted from *How to be a Nature Detective* by Millicent Selsam. Copyright © 1958, 1963 by Millicent Selsam. For "Magic Secrets," adapted from *Magic Secrets* by Rose Wyler and Gerald Ames. Copyright © 1967 by Gerald Ames and Rose Wyler. For an adaptation from *The Secret Language* by Ursula Nordstrom. Copyright © 1960 by Ursula Nordstrom. Used by permission.

Holiday House, for "Atu, the Silent One," adapted from *Atu, the Silent One* by Frank Jupo. Copyright © 1967 by Frank Jupo. Used by permission.

Holt, Rinehart and Winston, Publishers, for "Mr. Hare," a play based on *Mr. Hare* by Gardell Dano Christensen. Copyright © 1956 by Gardell Dano Christensen. There may be no performance of this play without written permission from the publisher. Used by permission.

Houghton Mifflin Company and Chatto & Windus, Ltd., for "Lovable Lyle," adapted from *Lovable Lyle* by Bernard Waber. Copyright © 1969 by Bernard Waber. Used by permission.

Lothrop, Lee & Shepard Co., Inc., for "Morning Arrow," adapted from *Morning Arrow* by Nanabah Chee Dodge. Copyright © 1975 by Nanabah Chee Dodge. Used by permission.

McIntosh and Otis, for "Whispers," from *Whispers and Other Poems* by Myra Cohn Livingston, published by Harcourt Brace Jovanovich, Inc. Copyright © 1958 by Myra Cohn Livingston. Used by permission.

Macmillan Publishing Co., Inc., for "Suppose I Were a Snowflake," by Trudy Abramchik. Compiled by Charles E. Schaefer and Kathleen C. Mellor. Copyright © 1971 by Center for Urban Education. Used by permission.

William Morrow & Company, Inc., for "The

Secret Box," adapted from *The Secret Box* by Joanna Cole. Copyright © 1971 by Joanna Cole. Used by permission.

Parents' Magazine Press, for "The Wisest Man in the World," adapted from *The Wisest Man in the World* by Benjamin Elkin. Copyright © 1968 by Benjamin Elkin. Used by permission.

Parents' Magazine Press and the author, for "Sound of Sunshine, Sound of Rain," excerpted from *Sound of Sunshine, Sound of Rain* by Florence Parry Heide. Copyright © 1970 by Florence Parry Heide. Used by permission.

G. P. Putnam's Sons, for "The Acrobats," from *All Together* by Dorothy Aldis. Copyright 1952 by Dorothy Aldis. Used by permission.

Scholastic Magazines, Inc., for "If You Lived With The Circus," adapted from *If You Lived With The Circus* by Ann McGovern. Copyright © 1971 by Ann McGovern. For "Hans Christian Andersen," adapted from *The Fairy Tale Life of Hans Christian Andersen* by Eva Moore.

Copyright © 1959 by Eva Moore. Used by permission.

Simon & Schuster, Inc., for "Singing," from *Miracles* by Richard Lewis. Copyright © 1966 by Simon & Schuster, Inc. Used by permission.

The Viking Press, Inc., for "Hattie, the Backstage Bat," adapted from *Hattie, the Backstage Bat* by Don Freeman. Copyright © 1970 by Don Freeman. Used by permission.

Barbara Brooks Wallace, for an adaptation of *Argyle*. Copyright © 1973 by Barbara Brooks Wallace. Used by permission.

Albert Whitman & Co., for "The Swinging Bridge," adapted from *Marcos, a Mountain Boy of Mexico* by Millicent Humason Lee. Used by permission.

Any material on evolution presented in this textbook is presented as theory rather than fact.

Art Credits:

Bernard Waber, pages 16 – 35
Ethel Gold, pages 36 – 45
Diane deGroat, pages 46 – 59, 69, 152, 184 – 191, 201, 220 – 221
Ed Frascino, pages 60 – 68
Richard Armundsen, pages 70 – 84
Blair Drawson, pages 85, 139
Colos, pages 86 – 95
Arthur Shilstone, pages 96 – 105
Sven Lindman, pages 106, 153, 210, 278, (career graphics)
Kenneth Longtemps, pages 106 – 107, 280 – 296
Jeannie Williams, pages 110 – 117
Jan Palmer, pages 118 – 126
Errol le Cain, pages 127, 312 – 323
Norman La Liberté, pages 128 – 138
Lawrence Di Fiori, pages 140 – 151

Patti Churchill, page 153
Norman Green, pages 154 – 166
Bob Goldstein, page 167
Charles Molina, pages 168 – 181
Tad Krumeich, pages 192, 258
Marie Michal, pages 202 – 209
Donald Bolognese, pages 210 – 211
Don Freeman, pages 212, 219
Bryant Weintraub, pages 248, 250, 251, 255
Carolyn Schumsky, page 249
Howard Schumsky, page 252
Holden Weintraub, pages 253, 254, 257
Denver Gillen, pages 259 – 265
Robert Van Nutt, pages 271, 274, 277
Len Ebert, pages 298 – 310
Tom Leigh, page 311
Melanie Arwin, pages 324 – 351

Cover art by Gil Cohen

Photo Credits:

p. 106 HRW Photos by Russell Dian. p. 107 top, Peter Barton; bottom, HRW Photo by Russell Dian. p. 153 Peter Schaaf. p. 210 – 211 Martha Swope. p. 222, 224 Brown Brothers. p. 225 left, Culver Pictures; right, Brown Brothers. p. 226 Culver Pictures. p. 228 top, top middle, bottom middle, Culver Pictures; bottom, Brown Brothers. p. 229 UPI. p. 230 Brown Brothers. p. 231 Jeanette Kehl. p. 232 top, Courtesy of Ringling Brothers Barnum & Bailey Combined Show, Inc.; bottom, Moos/Hake/Greenberg from Peter Arnold. p. 233 Elizabeth Corlett/dpi. p. 234 top, Dennis Stock/Magnum; bottom, Chuck Slade. p. 235 Marcia Keegan. p. 236 – 237 Elliott Erwitt. p. 238 left, Wayne Miller; right, Chuck Slade. p. 239, 241 Wayne Miller. p. 242 Dennis Stock. p. 243 Bruce Davidson. p. 244 Chuck Slade. p. 245 top, Wayne Miller; bottom, Chuck Slade. p. 266 – 267 Ingbet. p. 268 NYPL. p. 269 left, Library of Congress; right, NYPL. p. 271 NYPL. p. 272 Brown Brothers. p. 273 NYPL. p. 276 THE WORLD, 1/26/1890. p. 277 Brown Brothers. p. 278 Office of the U.S. Tre̶̶̶̶u. p. 279 UPI. p. 297 Ingbet.

Table of Contents

UNIT TWO
STORIES AND STORYTELLERS

UNIT THREE
ARTISTS AND PERFORMERS

UNIT FOUR
SPECIAL HAPPENINGS

1 WHISPERS AND SECRETS

Whispers

Whispers
   tickle through your ear
   telling you things you like to hear.

Whispers
   are as soft as skin
   letting little words curl in.

Whispers
   come so they can blow
   secrets others never know.

—Myra Cohn Livingston

Lovable Lyle

Bernard Waber

Everyone loved Lyle the Crocodile. The Primm family, with whom he lived, loved him dearly, of course. The woman who ran the bakery loved him. She always gave Lyle cookies. The man who sold ice cream loved him. He always invited Lyle to climb on his truck and ring the bell. Bird loved him. *"Love Lyle! Love Lyle!"* he called. And the children loved him. They always called for Lyle to come out and play.

In return, Lyle loved the whole, wide, wonderful world. He didn't have one enemy in it . . . or so he thought.

Then one day, quite mysteriously, a note addressed to Lyle was slid under the door of the house on East 88th Street. Mr. Primm read the note to Lyle.

Dear Lyle,

I don't like you. I don't like you at all.

Your enemy

Everyone was so surprised. *"Oh, how awful!"* cried Mrs. Primm. "Why would anyone not like Lyle?"

"Don't worry about it, Lyle," said Mr. Primm. "Just keep being your wonderful self, and try to forget this ever happened."

Lyle went off to bed that night trying hard to forget. Still, as he turned off the lights and looked down upon the quiet street below, he could not help sadly thinking,

The next day Lyle lost himself in play and forgot all about the note. But then a second one came as mysteriously as the first.

Dear Lyle,

I don't like you any more today than I did yesterday.

Your enemy

"Oh, these horrible notes have just got to stop!" Mrs. Primm cried out.

Lyle wanted the notes stopped, too. He was very unhappy about them. Some days he just wouldn't go out of the house. Other days he stayed outside being friendly to everyone. He did this so that somewhere, somehow, his *"enemy"* would see what a nice crocodile he really was. Lyle smiled a big, big smile. And he waved big, big waves, calling to one and all as friendly as he knew how.

He was kind and polite. He held doors open for people with heavy bundles. He shared his umbrella.

"My, isn't he polite!"
one woman said.

"I've never seen anything
like it," answered another.

Poor Lyle worked so hard at being nice that he was very tired by the end of the day.

One afternoon, Mrs. Primm, Joshua, and Lyle came across the words, "Down with all crocodiles," written on a fence near East 88th Street. Mrs. Primm tried to wash off the horrible words with her handkerchief.

"Well, Lyle," she said, as they made their way home, "it seems no matter how much we may think we want to, we can't always please everyone, or be liked by everyone."

As they got near their house, they noticed Clover Sue Hipple, a new girl in the neighborhood. By the time they reached their door, Clover was gone. Resting under the door was still another note addressed to Lyle.

"I just don't know if I can bring myself to read it," said Mrs. Primm. But she did.

Dear Lyle,

I wish you would go away and never come back — ever, ever again.

Your enemy

Sadly, Mrs. Primm tore up the note.

During the next few days, Mrs. Primm and Lyle found themselves running into Clover Sue Hipple almost everywhere they went. At the grocery they found her looking out from behind a large pile of potatoes.

Another time they caught sight of her behind a tree. And again one afternoon, they found her behind a mailbox.

Each time, Mrs. Primm smiled and tried to say hello. And each time, Clover ran off before Mrs. Primm got to her.

One day, as she was about to leave the house, Mrs. Primm looked down just in time to see another note being pushed under the door. Quickly, she opened the door. Before her, eyes wide with surprise, and still holding the note, stood Clover Sue Hipple.

"Clover dear, please don't run away," cried Mrs. Primm. "I would like to speak with you . . . about Lyle. Has Lyle done something to make you angry with him?"

"He takes my friends away from me," the little girl said. "When Lyle comes out, my friends

run away. They run to play with him. I never have any fun when Lyle is around."

"But why can't you play with Lyle, too?" asked Mrs. Primm.

"Because I'm not allowed. My mother said I'm not allowed ever to play with *crocodiles*," said Clover.

That night Mr. Primm said, "Why don't you ask Mrs. Hipple over here to meet Lyle? I'm sure when she sees for herself how gentle Lyle really is, she won't mind if Clover plays with him."

Mrs. Primm called Clover's mother the very next day. "Lyle and I want so much to meet you," she said. "Could you join us for tea to-morrow afternoon?"

"I would love to," answered Mrs. Hipple. She made a note of the address.

"Now who is this nice Mrs. Primm?" she wondered. "And who is Lyle?" The only Lyle she knew of was that awful crocodile, who lived with a strange family some-where nearby.

"Just think, a crocodile living right here in our neighborhood! This Lyle must be that nice Mrs. Primm's husband," she thought.

"Remember now, Lyle," said Mrs. Primm, the next afternoon, "be polite when Mrs. Hipple gets here. Take her coat. And when you have hung it in the closet, join us in the living room."

When Mrs. Hipple got there, Lyle started down the stairs to meet her. But then he stopped.

"What if she doesn't like me?" he thought. Suddenly Lyle became very shy. Suddenly the last thing in the world he wanted to do was meet Mrs. Hipple.

"Lyle! Lyle!" called Mrs. Primm. "Where are you? Mrs. Hipple is here." She led her guest into the living room.

Lyle wanted to go with her, but instead he squeezed himself into the hall closet and hid.

Over the tinkling of teacups, Lyle could hear the voices of the two women. They were talking about this, that, and everything under the sun. It was so stuffy in the closet, he began to wish they would talk about Mrs. Hipple going home soon.

At long last Lyle heard Mrs. Hipple say, "I must be going now." And Mrs. Primm said, "I'm so glad you came, and so sorry you missed Lyle, but I'm sure you will be meeting him soon." Then Lyle heard the handle of the closet door turn as Mrs. Primm said, "Here, let me get your coat."

The second the door opened, Lyle fell out upon the two women. Mrs. Primm gasped. And Mrs. Hipple yelled.

"Are you all right? Are you all right?" Mrs. Primm cried out, as they got to their feet.

"LET ME OUT OF HERE!"
Mrs. Hipple cried.
"LET ME OUT OF
THIS HORRIBLE HOUSE!"

Mrs. Primm opened the door as Mrs. Hipple, her hair and clothes all a mess, ran from the house. "If that crocodile ever so much as crosses my path, I'll have him put in jail," she called back over her shoulder.

"Poor Lyle," Mrs. Primm said that night. "Now he's afraid he's going to be put in jail. We're just going to have to think of something to take his mind off his troubles."

On the first warm day, Mr. and Mrs. Primm
knew just what to do for Lyle. "We'll take him
to the beach," they thought.

Lyle always loved to swim. And he could
swim better than anyone in the family.

While Mr. and Mrs. Primm sat down on the beach, and Joshua started on a sand castle, Lyle took a running jump into the water.

Lyle's water tricks made everyone laugh, everyone, that is, but Mrs. Hipple who was there with Clover.

Mrs. Hipple set out at once to find a life-guard.

"Lifeguard! Lifeguard!" she cried. "Are crocodiles allowed to swim here?"

"Of course not," answered the lifeguard.

"Well, there is a crocodile out there, this very minute." Mrs. Hipple showed him where she had seen the crocodile.

Suddenly, everyone was looking at a little girl bobbing about in the water.

"Clover! Clover!" cried Mrs. Hipple. "She's going to drown!"

At once the lifeguard pushed off to save her. But Lyle raced to Clover before him.

"There's a crocodile!" someone gasped.

"No, it's Lyle," called Mrs. Primm, standing nearby. "I mean it's Lyle the Crocodile."

Lyle brought a very wet, but happy Clover safely back to shore.

"Oh, Lyle, dear friend," sobbed Mrs. Hipple, "how can I ever thank you enough?"

Everyone was so proud of Lyle. He was made an honorary lifeguard and given a hat and a silver whistle.

"Lyle, you are very brave," said the head lifeguard. "Feel free to come here and save people whenever you want."

The next day a note addressed to Lyle was found under the door of the house on East 88th Street. "Not again!" Mrs. Primm cried. Mr. Primm read the note.

Dear Lyle,

I love you. I love you more than anything. I love you so much I can't stand it.

Your friend for life,

Clover Sue Hipple

P.S. May I play with you today?
P.P.S. My mother said it was all right.

Reflections

1. Why did so many people love Lyle?
2. Why did Clover Sue Hipple dislike Lyle?
3. Why did Lyle try to be friendly to everyone after he received the notes?
4. Why did Clover change her mind about Lyle?
5. Would you like Lyle to be your friend? Why or why not?
6. Write a note telling Lyle what you think of him. Follow the form of the note used in the story.

THE SECRET BOX

Joanna Cole

Ann Marie was a city kid. She lived in a housing project in New York. From the kitchen window, she could see ten floors down.

Ann Marie's father and mother worked, so there was always some job for her to do. When she came home from school, she had to clean up the house and watch her two sisters. At dinnertime her mother would say, "Ann Marie, we need some bread from the store," or, "Haven't you set the table yet?"

Ann Marie never seemed to have any time of her own. She hardly ever got to visit Vanessa, her best friend in school. Instead she had to stay with her little sisters. Sometimes they had fun together. But Ann Marie didn't like to be with little kids all the time.

Ann Marie wanted to have something all to herself. So she made a secret box, which she kept under her bed. It was only a small box, but it was big enough to hold a picture of her class, some pretty buttons, and a few other things she liked to collect.

Sometimes when it rained, Ann Marie took out her things and looked at them. She put all the buttons on a string and made a necklace. Or she picked out the kids she liked best in the picture. She made sure her sisters never knew about her box because then it wouldn't be a secret anymore. Ann Marie never told *anyone* about the secret box.

One day Ann Marie was standing near Mr. Freeman's desk. Mr. Freeman was the best teacher she had ever had. Almost everyone in the class liked him.

On Mr. Freeman's desk was a pencil that was red on one end and blue on the other. Ann Marie looked at it for a long time. She looked around the room and saw that no one was looking at her. She picked up the pencil and put it in her pocket. It would be wonderful for the secret box.

The next morning, as she got ready for school, Ann Marie began to wonder if Mr. Freeman knew she had taken the pencil. At breakfast she was very quiet.

"What's the matter, Ann Marie?" her father asked.

"Nothing," she said. But there was something the matter. Ann Marie was afraid that Mr. Freeman would be mad at her.

When she got to school, everything was all right. Mr. Freeman asked her to clean the blackboards, as he always did. She saw another red and blue pencil on his desk. Ann Marie guessed Mr. Freeman had a lot of pencils. "He didn't even notice it was gone," she thought.

On the way to lunch Vanessa said, "This afternoon we're going to gym. Maybe Mrs. Miller will let us be on the same side, Ann Marie."

"Maybe," Ann Marie said. "But I don't think so. She's too mean."

Luis was behind Ann Marie. He always liked to tease her.

"Ann Marie can't even hit a volleyball over the net," he said.

"I can hit it better than you," Ann Marie said.

"Ann Marie, Luis," said Mr. Freeman. "There is no talking in line."

After lunch the class went to gym. Mrs. Miller, the gym teacher, wouldn't let you play if you talked in line. So everyone tried to come in quietly.

Today Luis whispered, *"Ann Marie can't hit a ball,"* and pushed her hard into the kids in front of her.

"You stop it!" Ann Marie said.

Just then Mrs. Miller turned around. *"Ann Marie!"* she shouted. "No gym for you today! Sit on the bench!"

Ann Marie watched Luis playing with a big smile on his face. She felt like crying. She was so mad she didn't watch the game. Instead she looked down at the floor, where all the kids had put their books.

"I wish I never had to see Mrs. Miller's face again," Ann Marie thought. She gave Mrs. Miller a look that said, "I'm mad at you!" Then she gave Luis one, too, but he didn't see it.

She looked down and saw a pencil case was next to her foot. Inside the case Ann Marie could see a gold ring with a blue stone. If she had that ring in the secret box, she wouldn't care about Mrs. Miller or Luis or volleyball anymore. Slowly Ann Marie reached down, took the ring out, and put it in her sneaker.

Mrs. Miller blew the whistle. Ann Marie went over and stood by the door while the other kids got their books.

"Don't worry, Ann Marie," Vanessa said. "I bet Luis only acts that way because he likes you."

"I don't care," Ann Marie said. "I'm mad at him!"

That night Ann Marie put the ring in her secret box. It looked even better than the red and blue pencil. She put it on her finger and took it off again. It made her feel pretty. Then she heard her sister coming into the room, so she dropped the ring in the box and slid the box under the bed.

"I wonder who the ring belongs to," she thought, as she went to sleep.

The next day Ann Marie got to school just before the bell rang. She took out her homework and handed Vanessa a piece of gum under the desk. Vanessa didn't take it.

"Vanessa," she whispered. "Here's some gum."

"I don't feel like any," Vanessa said.

"What's the matter?" Ann Marie saw that her friend's eyes were red. "Have you been crying?"

"Someone took my ring," Vanessa said.

Ann Marie felt awful.

"I only got it yesterday," Vanessa said, "and today it's gone."

"Maybe you lost it," Ann Marie said.

"No, I didn't," Vanessa said, and her face looked hard.

"Maybe it'll turn up," Ann Marie said. Then she was quiet. She knew that she had taken Vanessa's ring.

All day in school Ann Marie felt bad. When three o'clock came, it was raining hard. She walked through the water on the way home and got her shoes wet. All the other kids had umbrellas. Ann Marie felt so bad she didn't even care if she got wet.

After supper, Ann Marie helped in the kitchen. Then she went to bed early. She didn't look in the secret box. She didn't do her homework. She just closed her eyes and tried to forget what she had done.

The next morning she went to school early. She was the first one there. She sat down at her desk and took the ring and the red and blue pencil out of her bag. Slowly she put the ring in Vanessa's desk and the pencil on Mr. Freeman's. Soon the other kids came in.

Ann Marie went to sharpen her pencil. As she passed Luis's desk, she saw a new roll of play money. She stopped and looked at it. "I wonder if it would fit in the secret box," she thought.

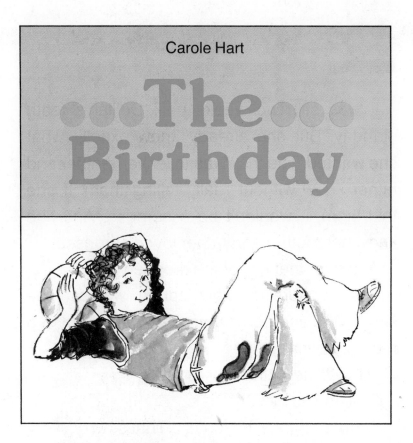

Carole Hart

The Birthday

Delilah Bush is almost ten years old.
She's the tallest girl in her class.
She plays basketball and drums.

She has two left feet. (They're made of green felt, and they're sewn to the back of her favorite pair of blue jeans.)

She also has short, very curly hair. It's brown-red in winter, red-brown in summer.

One of Delilah's eyes is gray. The other is gray-green.

It was still two weeks until Delilah's tenth birthday. But she already knew exactly what she wanted. The trick was to let her mother and father know without really telling them. If she told them, it wouldn't be a surprise. And she knew her mother and father loved surprises.

At dinner that night, she dropped a hint.

"We're studying how sound works," she said. "We learned how you get sound out of a record player. It's very, very interesting."

"How?" her father asked.

Delilah told him.

"You're right," he said. "That's very, very interesting."

A few nights later, they all went shopping together. Delilah stopped at a record bin and began thumbing through it. The bin was packed with all kinds of records.

Her mother said, "We'll meet you in Housewares."

And they left her thumbing.

A salesclerk came over.

"May I help you?" he asked Delilah.

"Just looking," Delilah said.

Slowly she made her way to Housewares. There she found her mother and father buying garbage bags.

In the car on the way home, Delilah tried again. She asked her father what his favorite kind of music was.

"All kinds," he said.

"I guess I like rock best," her mother said.

"Me, too," said Delilah.

"OK. I get it," her father said.

Then he turned the radio to a rock station.

Delilah wasn't so sure her father got it.

The next week she borrowed a record of *Peter and the Wolf* from the library.

"Why?" her mother said.

"Because I like it," Delilah answered. "And in a minute I'm going over to Jenny's to listen to it."

"Too bad you don't have your own record player," her mother said.

Delilah closed her book. She watched her mother sew a patch on an old pair of her blue jeans.

"Would you mind picking up some milk on the way home?" her mother said.

Delilah didn't mind at all. In fact, she was very happy. Her mother had guessed what she wanted for her tenth birthday. She didn't need to drop another hint.

All she had to do was wait. But the suspense was hard to bear.

Finally her birthday arrived.

She got seven out of ten wrong on a spelling test. She wasn't listening when her teacher called out the words.

Then she was asked a question she couldn't answer. She just didn't hear it.

It would have been an awful day, except it was her birthday.

When Delilah got home from school, her mother and father were waiting for her. They had come home from work early.

"Happy birthday, Delilah!" they said both at the same time.

"Thank you," Delilah said, biting her lip. She could hardly stand the suspense.

"We have a present for you," her father said, "in your room."

Delilah rushed off to her room. When she got there, she stopped short. She was very surprised.

Curled up in the middle of her bed was a puppy — sleeping.

"Oh!" Delilah said.

The puppy opened his eyes and looked at her, without raising his head.

Delilah loved him at once and forever. She called him Hi-Fido.

Delilah Bush is just ten years old. But she likes to say she's going on eleven.

Sometimes she dreams about what she wants for other birthdays. Or she dreams about what she would like to do.

When she's really eleven, she would like to have a record player.

In two years (or maybe three) she wants a minibike.

When she's sixteen, she wants to visit her cousin in California.

Tomorrow she has to go to the dentist. She will tell her all about Hi-Fido.

Reflections

1. What hints did Delilah give to tell her parents what she wanted for her birthday?
2. Why didn't Delilah do well on the spelling test?
3. Why do you think Delilah's parents gave her a puppy for her birthday?
4. Do you think Delilah wanted a record player more than a puppy? Why or why not?
5. Write a description of a real or imaginary friend. Use the description on page 61 to help you.

The Wind
Came Running

The Wind came running
over the sand,
it caught and held me
by the hand.

It curled and whirled
and danced with me
down to the edge
of the dashing sea.

We danced together,
the Wind and I,
to the cry of a gull
and a wild sea cry.

—Ivy O. Eastwick

How to Be a Nature Detective

Millicent Selsam

"What happened here?" a detective asks. "Who was here? Where did he go?"

A detective has many ways to find out.

One way is to look for the marks someone or something has made—fingerprints, footprints, the tracks made by car tires.

Sometimes a detective finds a hair or a button. These things are clues. They help a detective answer these questions: What happened? Who was here? Where did he go?

You can be a detective, too, a special kind of detective—a nature detective.

Nature detectives find tracks and clues that answer *these* questions:

What animal walked here?
Where did it go?
What did it do?
What did it eat?

Where does a nature detective look for clues? Almost anywhere — in a backyard, in the woods, in a city park.

You can find tracks in many places — in mud, in snow, in sand, in dust, even on the sidewalk or on the floor.

Wet feet or wet muddy paws can make a track anywhere.

Here is a mystery for a nature detective:

Here is a dish for a cat
and a dish for a dog.

The cat's dish had milk in it.

The dog's dish had meat in it.

Who drank the milk?
Who ate the meat?
Look at the tracks and see.

Look at the tracks that go to the *cat's* dish. They were made by an animal that walks on four feet. And you see claw marks.

A cat has four feet and sharp claws. But so does a dog.

Who went to the cat's dish? We still don't know. Let's look for more clues.

Now look at the other tracks—the tracks that go to the *dog's* dish.

Did you ever watch a cat walk? A cat walks on four feet. But the tracks of its hind feet fall right on top of the tracks of its front feet. So its footprints are one behind the other, in one line.

They look like the footprints of an animal with only two legs.

A cat pulls its claws in when it walks. That is why it does not leave claw marks.

Now do you know who drank the milk?
Who ate the dog food?

Tigers and other big cats make tracks in a line, just like a house cat.

Most of you won't be tracking tigers. But you may see fox tracks.

The footprints of a fox are in one line, like a cat's footprints. But they have claw marks, like a dog's.

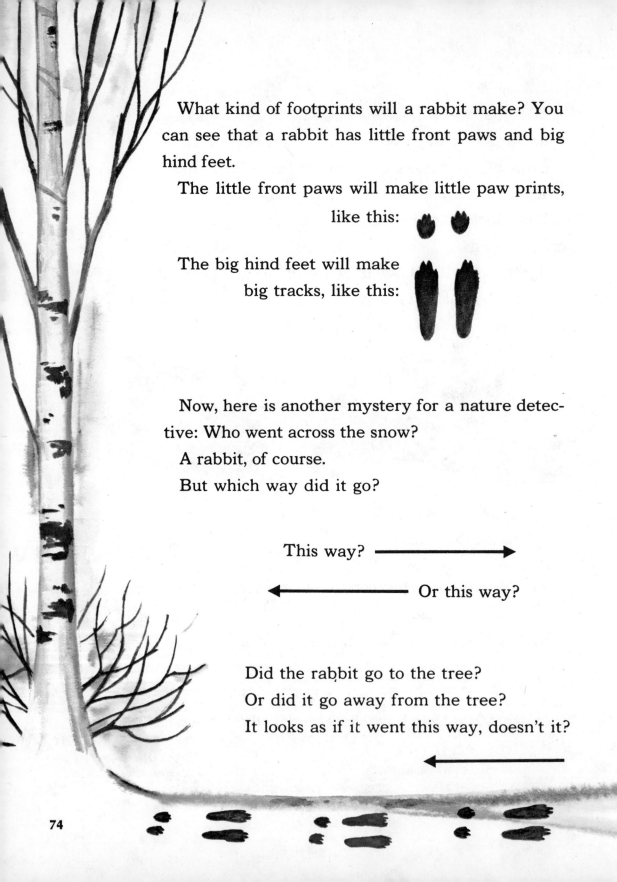

What kind of footprints will a rabbit make? You can see that a rabbit has little front paws and big hind feet.

The little front paws will make little paw prints, like this:

The big hind feet will make big tracks, like this:

Now, here is another mystery for a nature detective: Who went across the snow?

A rabbit, of course.

But which way did it go?

This way? ⟶

⟵ Or this way?

Did the rabbit go to the tree?

Or did it go away from the tree?

It looks as if it went this way, doesn't it?

You can see the marks of the front paws ahead of the big hind feet.

But do you know how a rabbit jumps? Look at that!

When a rabbit jumps, it puts its big hind feet ahead of its front paws.

What happened here on a snowy day?

You can see the rabbit tracks in the snow. You know that they are going this way. ⟶

All at once the rabbit tracks are far apart. That means the rabbit began to take big jumps. It was in a hurry. Why?

Do you see those tracks coming out of the woods? Those footprints have claw marks like a dog's. But they are in one line, like the tracks of a cat.

Who could have made those tracks? There is only one answer . . .

A fox!

Now you know why the rabbit was in a hurry! Did the fox catch the rabbit? Look again.

There are big hoofprints in the mud near the river. And there are little hoofprints, too. Who was here?

It was a mother deer and her baby. They came to the river for water.

Somebody sat down on the muddy bank of the river. Who?

These back footprints were
made by webbed feet.

This is the mark of a round fat belly.

A frog came out of the river. It sat on the muddy bank to rest.

And somebody made these tracks that go right into the water.

Only a snake leaves tracks like this. A snake came down to the river. Then it slid into the water.

Here are more tracks in the mud near the river. And there is a little pile of shells, too. They are crayfish shells.

The tracks look something like the hands and feet of a baby. But look at those long claws! A raccoon made those tracks. Raccoons like to catch crayfish.

So now you know what happened.

A raccoon had dinner here last night. It found crayfish in the river. It ate the crayfish. And it left the shells in a little pile.

A nature detective can find many clues on a sandy beach.

When you walk on the beach in the morning, look for the sea-gull tracks. They can tell you which way the wind was blowing when the sea gulls were there.

Like airplanes, sea gulls take off into the wind. First the gulls must run along the sand to get up speed for a take-off. As they run, their toes dig deeper into the sand.

Here all the sea gull toe tracks are in a line toward the west. So you know that the wind came from the west.

Tracks are good clues for a nature detective. But there are other clues, too.

A nature detective must learn to look and listen—and smell.

The detective can find clues in a backyard, in the woods, or in a city park.

Who went by?

Who ate here?

Who lives here?

What's going on here?

This is what's going on!

Reflections

1. What clues should a nature detective look for?
2. Write a story telling what you would do to be the best nature detective in the world.

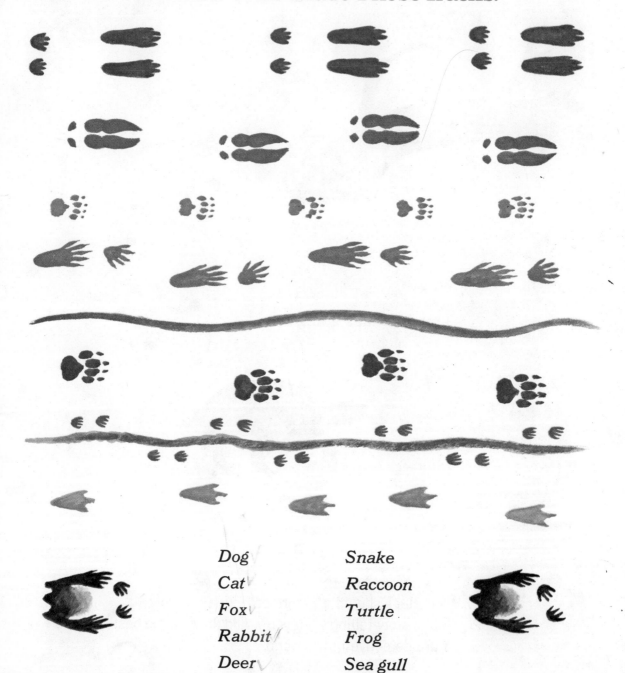

Do You Know Who Made These Tracks?

Dog   Snake

Cat   Raccoon

Fox   Turtle

Rabbit   Frog

Deer   Sea gull

Footprints

In summertime
it's hard to know
where dogs
and mice
and rabbits go:
Their grassy footprints
never show—
you can't tell where
they lead.

In wintertime
there's little doubt
where wild and tame ones
run about:
Their snowy footprints
write it out...
and I know how to read!

—Aileen Fisher

85

Jill Wants SUNGLASSES

Elizabeth Levy

If there was one thing Jill wanted, it was sunglasses. **Big sunglasses!** No one in Jill's class had sunglasses. Her sister didn't own a pair and neither did her father or mother.

But Jill wanted sunglasses, and she was getting to be something of a pest. It began just before Christmas of last year.

"If anyone wants to know what to give me," Jill said to her mother, "I can tell them."

Her mother just laughed and told Jill that she had already bought her a Christmas gift. Jill didn't get sunglasses for Christmas. She got a model spaceship set instead.

Spring came, and Jill still wanted sunglasses. Her birthday was May 5. She made up her mind to come right out with it.

"Mom," she said, "I want sunglasses."

Her mother gave her a funny look and said, "Birthday gifts are nicer when they're a surprise."

"But Mom," said Jill.

"Never mind," said her mother.

That night Jill's older sister, Laura, talked to Jill alone in their room.

"I wish you'd stop this sunglasses stuff," Laura said. "A joke is a joke. But you've got Mom and Dad really worried. And if you don't stop, everyone will start thinking something is the matter with you. Now I'm your sister, and I know you're a little strange. But I don't want other people to think so."

"I'm not joking, and I don't see anything strange about wanting sunglasses," Jill said. She started to get very red in the face.

"You're blushing," said Laura, who loved to tease her sister.

"I am not," said Jill, who hated to be caught blushing.

"You are, too," said Laura.

"I'm **not!**" shouted Jill, still blushing. And she picked up her pillow and threw it at Laura.

Laura was about to throw it back when the girls' mother came into the room and told them to grow up.

On May 5 Jill had a birthday party. Her friends in the building came with gifts. One friend brought a model of a grocery store, where people used to buy real food long ago.

It was a good party. They were allowed twenty minutes to make noise.

They had plenty of candy and cake cubes to eat.

But there were no sunglasses for Jill.

That night, Jill lay in her bed thinking. She knew that having sunglasses was a silly idea. She didn't need them. Jill thought it was time to forget about sunglasses.

Summer came. Jill's family got to take a trip to the national park.

The trip was very exciting. It was the first time Jill had been out of her building in over a year. First the family took the elevator down 240 floors to the ground. Next they went into the room where they picked up their oxygen masks. Then they went outside.

It was quite a bit darker out there than it was inside the building. Inside, where Jill and her family lived, bright lights were everywhere. Outside there was only a gray light. It was hard to get used to.

Every family in Jill's building took a trip to the national park once a year. The government spent a lot of money keeping the park going. There were maple trees and evergreens, flowers, and even crickets.

Nobody ate food cubes on vacation. The government had real food on hand. If you went fishing and caught any fish, you could cook them yourself.

On the third day of their vacation, Jill's family split up for the afternoon. Jill's mother and Laura took the wild flower field trip. Jill and her father went fishing.

Jill and her father had gone fishing on their vacation last year. They had had a great time. They had been able to talk all by themselves. That was something they did not get to do very much at home.

This year, they had been fishing about an hour and not catching much when Jill's father said, "There's something I've been wanting to ask you."

"What's that?" asked Jill.

"Well, remember all your talk about sunglasses?" asked Jill's dad.

"Sure," said Jill. "I still kind of want them, even if all of you thought I was being silly."

"But that's what I wanted to ask," said her father. "What are sunglasses?"

"You must be joking," said Jill. "I thought you and Mom had them when you were young."

"I've never heard of them," said Jill's father. "That's why we were so worried. We thought you made it up."

"No," said Jill. "Sunglasses are real. I saw a picture of them in an old book. It showed how people lived in the 1970's. There were people at the beach and the sun was out. Most of the people had dark glasses on. The book said they were sunglasses, and that people wore them because the sun was too bright."

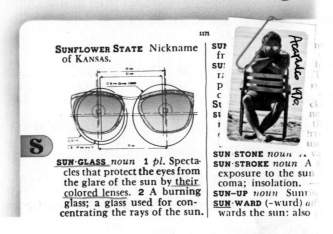

"Well," said Jill's father. "That really is something. Imagine! The sun was too bright!"

"Sunglasses are great-looking," said Jill, getting excited. "I thought it would be fun to have a pair."

"You know," said Jill's father, "I remember that my grandfather used to talk about bright sunlight when I was a kid. He said the sun was so bright that sometimes you had to blink. I had forgotten all about that."

"Wasn't there any bright sun when you were a kid?"asked Jill.

"No," said Jill's father. "It was brighter than it is now, of course. People talked about cleaning up the air. And we didn't have to wear oxygen masks outside. Still the sun wasn't what you'd call bright even then."

"So you never had sunglasses?" asked Jill.

"Never," said Jill's dad. "Do you still have that book with the picture in it?"

"Sure," said Jill. "It's at home."

"I'd like to see it," said Jill's dad.

When they got back from their vacation, Jill showed her mother and father the book. Jill's father couldn't get over the idea of sunglasses. It seemed so funny to him.

"Say," he said, "let's find out how to make them."

The next day Jill and her father took the elevator to the library and read all about sunglasses. They found out that sunglasses are made of colored glass. Colored glass kept the bright sunlight of long ago from hurting people's eyes. They also found out that sunglasses came in different colors and shapes. People could pick the color and shape they wanted.

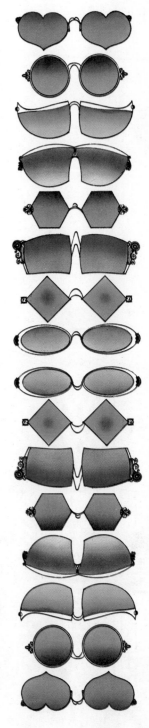

The more they read, the more they wanted sunglasses. But Jill's father had given up the idea of making them. He had a better idea.

"Jill," he said. "Mr. Arnold works at the glass works. He loves colored glass. He's always making things out of it. He's our man. Let's go down the hall to see him."

Jill's father was right. Mr. Arnold not only made the sunglasses for them, he made them in different colors and shapes. He even made a pair for himself.

When the glasses were ready, Jill and her family put them on, went out into the hall, and walked to the elevator. Everyone they passed, stopped to give them a second look. All that week they went around their building wearing sunglasses.

It was fun, but it was only a joke. All their friends thought they were being very silly. In the year 2275, nobody in the world needed sunglasses.

Reflections

1. Why did the family in this story wear sunglasses?
2. What clues tell you this is a fanciful story?
3. How is the food described in this story different from today's food?
4. Do you think people will live this way in 2275? Why or why not?
5. What gift from the past would you like? Why?
6. Reread page 88. Write a story about a real or make-believe birthday party.

Kiya the Gull

Fen H. Lasell

Kiya was a free bird. From dawn to sundown he would sweep the sky, the sand, and the sea, looking for food. He kept a close eye on the harbor to pick up after fishermen. On the beach he watched the children and ate sandwiches they couldn't finish. Like all sea gulls, he was willing to eat almost anything.

Kiya began the day at dawn. He left the little island where he lived and went right to the harbor. He wanted to be there when the fishermen came in to clean their fish.

This morning no fishermen were in, but the sea had left on the rocky beach a bundle of seaweed, crabs, and snails—all tangled in wire.

Kiya flew around the bundle. When he had found it quite safe, he went to work. He had to pick out the seaweed to reach the snails and crabs. But the wire kept getting in his way.

Kiya had to tug at the wire until one end came free. Then he put his head in the opening and pulled out the seaweed.

Other gulls, hungry for breakfast, joined him. They pulled at the wire and picked out the seaweed. They ate what they could. They flew away with snails in their bills to break the hard shells by dropping them on rocks.

When the party was over, Kiya found that now it was he who was tangled in the wire.

"Kiya-kiya-kiya," he cried.

The harder Kiya tried to free himself, the tighter the wire pulled. At last he freed his wings, but a loop of wire bound his back and one leg so tightly that he could not move it.

A boy was sitting in his boat watching the gulls. When he saw Kiya's trouble, he got out and ran toward the bird. The frightened Kiya flapped his wings and rose out of reach, even though the wire cut into his back and leg.

The bird glided over to the sandy beach and made a clumsy landing on one foot. He hopped along the cool, hard sand near the water, dragging part of the wire that bound him.

People were already gathering on the beach for a day in the sun.

"Look at the sea gull!" someone called. "He's all tangled up in something."

People ran toward Kiya. Hands reached out for him. Beating his wings, Kiya managed to raise himself again.

He flew to the high dune where the sea gulls perch at noon. The other gulls were still away looking for their morning meal. Hungry as Kiya was, it hurt him too much to fly. He wanted only to be left in peace.

Then children came to climb the dune and slide down the warm sand.

"Look!" one cried. "That sea gull is all tangled up. Let's catch him!"

Kiya watched the children come closer and closer. He spread his wings and tried to fly. At last he rose out of their reach.

Kiya landed on the water. The cool waves washed his cuts. He bobbed on the waves and let them draw him out to sea. How was he going to get rid of the wire? How was he going to find something to eat?

Suddenly, there was that boy again, heading toward him in his boat. Kiya tried to swim away. But with only one leg, it was hard to keep from going round and round.

Kiya saw two hands reaching for him. He beat his wings to raise himself away from the hands. Once more he was safe in the air.

Where could he go but back to his island? There were too many people on the mainland forever trying to catch him. In all his life no one had ever tried to catch him. Why now, when he was in pain?

Kiya landed on his perch. At first the other gulls gave him his place on the roof of the old shack. But when they saw his cuts, they no longer wanted him around. He was not one of them. He was tangled and hurt.

A gull flying in pushed him. Then all at once the gulls turned on him and drove him to the ground. Dragging his wire behind, Kiya hopped away and hid in the tall grass.

When evening brought still more gulls, Kiya hopped to the other side of the island. Then as he was trying to get to the top of a sand dune, his wire caught on a bush, and he was held fast.

The sun was low in the west when the boat came in sight, bringing the boy to the island. Kiya watched the boy wade ashore and then turn and walk away from him along the beach.

Kiya was well hidden where he was. If he didn't move, the boy would never find him, and soon it would be dark.

But the boy came back and built a fire on the beach, just below the bush where Kiya was caught. The bird watched the flames until at last he fell asleep.

During the night Kiya woke to find the fire still burning low. At dawn the fire had gone out, but the boy was still asleep in his sleeping bag. Now was the time for Kiya to get away, before the boy woke and found him. He threw his weight against the wire and beat his poor lame wings against the bush. "Kiya-kiya-kiya," he cried.

The uproar woke the boy. He climbed the hill and stood above Kiya. They looked at one another, bird and boy. Kiya knew his time had come. He opened his bill to bite at the reaching hand, but the boy closed it over his head.

"Easy now!" said the boy as he tried to free the bird from the wire.

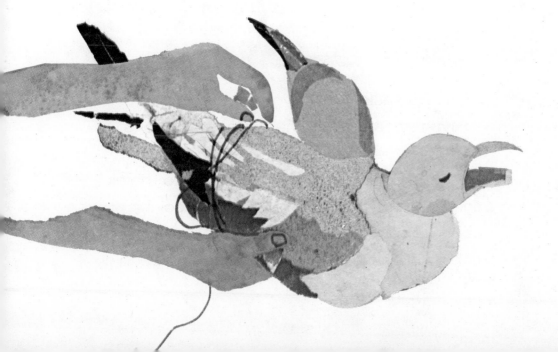

Kiya gave up trying to fight and lay still. At last the boy was able to lift the loop of wire from the bird's back and to wind it off his leg. Then two hands lifted him gently and set him on his feet.

Kiya tried to take a step. He limped, but he could walk. The bird could not believe what had happened. He looked at the boy standing over him. The hands that had freed him from the wire were no longer reaching for him.

The boy asked, "Will you be all right?"

Kiya felt free. When he flapped his wings, there was no cutting wire. Though he was weak, he could fly. Slowly he rose into the air and flew around the boy, who was looking up at him. Then he glided down to the water to bob awhile on the waves. Why had he been so frightened of the boy with the reaching hands?

All summer Kiya flew over the harbor and the beach. There were many boys. There were many boats. Was there one there who had freed him from the wire?

And the boy with the boat looked up and wondered, of all those sea gulls gliding above, was there one he knew? Which was the gull he had saved?

Reflections

1. What do sea gulls like to eat?
2. Why did the gulls drop the snails on rocks?
3. Why was Kiya surprised that so many people were trying to catch him?
4. Why did the other gulls want to get rid of Kiya?
5. Do you think the boy ever saw Kiya again? Why or why not?
6. Make a list of some of the ways we can help wild animals live longer.

Home Arts

Have you ever used a recipe to make cookies? Have you helped pin a pattern on a piece of cloth? Have you ever read the directions for using a new household tool? If so, you've used the services of people in the home economics field. Perhaps some day you would like to work in that field. You could choose from all kinds of jobs that help people in their lives at home.

This food editor for a magazine is putting together a tasty salad. When she's finished, she'll write the recipe for the magazine's readers. What's the secret of her best recipes? They're easy to prepare, good to eat, and not too expensive. And the readers like that!

Is the material of the clothes you are wearing rough or smooth? Is it heavy or light? Are the threads woven in a design or is the material plain? These are questions that a fabric designer decides. Here we see a fabric designer who recently received his degree in textile design. He is examining several garments to determine if the pattern fits the style. Whatever he decides, the results will be good, for he is an expert.

This director of consumer affairs and her assistant work for a large company. But they also work for the people who use their company's products. They solve problems and provide information for the consumer. To do their job, they must understand people and their needs. Then, they can tell their company when its products fail to meet these needs. This information helps the company make better products.

2 STORIES AND STORYTELLERS

Which Is the Way to Somewhere Town?

Which is the way to Somewhere Town?
  Oh, up in the morning early;
Over the tiles and the chimney pots,
  That is the way, quite clearly.

And which is the door to Somewhere Town?
  Oh, up in the morning early;
The round red sun is the door to go through,
  That is the way, quite clearly.

— Kate Greenaway

Argyle

Barbara Brooks Wallace

Once upon a time, in Scotland, there was a sheep named Argyle.

Argyle was just like all the other sheep. He looked like a sheep. And he felt like a sheep. He liked to do the same things other sheep did. He wasn't one bit different from any of them.

When the sheep were together, MacDougal, the sheepherder, couldn't tell Argyle from the others. "A sheep is a sheep," MacDougal always said.

That was all right with Argyle. It was just the way he wanted it.

All day, Argyle roamed the highlands and the lowlands and the middle lands with the other sheep. It was nice and quiet. It was just the way he wanted it.

All sheep like to go around in groups. So did Argyle. But once in a while a sheep likes to roam away. So did Argyle. He didn't do it very often. He just did it sometimes.

One day he roamed away. He came to a strange place behind some tall rocks. The grass there tasted good. Argyle also liked the pretty little flowers there. He liked the way the red and blue and white and green and purple and yellow flowers tasted. In fact, he thought they were very good.

Argyle didn't tell anyone about them. But he went back the next day. And he went back the day after. And he went back the day after that. He ate hundreds of the little colored flowers.

One day MacDougal's wife, Katharine, said,
"Why dinna ye tell me about the many-colored
sheep, MacDougal?"

"Because we do na have a many-colored
sheep, Katharine," said MacDougal.

"Look again," said Katharine.

MacDougal looked again. Indeed there was
a many-colored sheep. It was red and blue and
white and green and purple and yellow.

The sheep was Argyle.

MacDougal ran for his shears and started cutting. Katharine ran for her knitting needles and started knitting. Soon she finished. Then they both ran to show all their friends the beautiful colored socks.

Well! You can imagine how important Argyle would be in Scotland. All the people there wanted to see him.

It didn't take MacDougal long to decide that Argyle should not be roaming around. So he put him in a pen where he was all alone. Hundreds of people came. They paid a lot of money to see him. And they paid a lot of money to buy his wool, too.

Soon MacDougal and Katharine grew very rich.

Mayor Loch of Lomond even came and gave Argyle a medal.

But Argyle didn't feel like a sheep anymore. He didn't like all the attention. It was never nice and quiet. He couldn't roam the highlands and the lowlands and the middle lands. And, of course, he couldn't get back to the place where the pretty colored flowers grew.

So he started to turn sheep color again.

MacDougal was so worried that he fed Argyle all kinds of special food. Argyle didn't like that. He became unhappy. He stopped *feeling* like a sheep. And he stopped *looking* like one, too. Soon all his wool fell out.

Well! It didn't take long for the people to stop coming around. Mayor Loch of Lomond came. But he only came to take away the medal. He couldn't take away the money MacDougal and Katharine had made. So they stayed rich the rest of their lives.

Katharine kept right on knitting. She finally discovered how to make colored socks out of dyed wool. She called them argyle socks, of course. You may have heard of them.

MacDougal finally gave up on Argyle. He sent him out with the rest of the sheep.

Argyle grew back his old sheep coat. Soon you couldn't tell him from anybody else. He looked like a sheep. And he felt like a sheep again.

If Argyle ever went back to the place with the pretty colored flowers, he never told anyone. He stayed his old sheep color. So you can be sure he wasn't eating anything but the grass.

He just roamed the highlands and the lowlands and the middle lands with all the other sheep. It was nice and quiet. It was just the way he wanted it.

Reflections

1. How often did Argyle like to roam away?
2. How did MacDougal and Katharine get rich?
3. Why didn't Argyle like all the attention?
4. Why did MacDougal feed Argyle special food?
5. If you were Argyle, would you have wanted to stay your old sheep color? Why or why not?
6. Pretend you are Argyle. Write how you feel about being the most important sheep in Scotland.

Lore Segal

Mitzi and the President

"Play with me," Martha said to her father.

"I'm reading," said her father.

"I'm hungry," said Martha.

Martha's father put down his book. He got up and made Martha a piece of bread and butter. Then he sat down and picked up his book.

"And I'm thirsty," said Martha.

Martha's father put down his book. He got up and brought Martha a glass of milk. Then he sat down and picked up his book.

"Tell me a Mitzi," Martha said.

Once upon a time (said her father) there was a father, and he had a little girl called Mitzi, and she had a brother called Jacob. Mitzi and Jacob and their father all went for a walk.

Mitzi said, "I'm hungry for some gum."

Jacob said, "Me, too."

Their father said, "I don't have any."

"Well, I want some," said Mitzi. "Please."

"Me, too," said Jacob.

"Well, I don't have any," said his father.

"Look in your pocket, please," said Mitzi.

Mitzi's father looked in his left jacket pocket and in his right jacket pocket. He looked in his breast pocket and in his two trouser pockets. Then he said, "No. No gum. Besides, the sugar is bad for your teeth. And when that's gone you don't want to chew the gum anymore. You don't even like chewing gum."

"Yes, I do," said Mitzi, "and so does Jacob."

So their father took them to buy chewing gum, but the shop was closed. It had a notice up : GONE TO THE PARADE.

"I want a parade," yelled Jacob.

"Me, too!" said Mitzi.

"Me, too!" said Mitzi's father.

A lot of people were running, and Mitzi's father and Mitzi and Jacob ran too. Then the first motorcycle went past, and behind it came two more. One was on the left and one on the right side of the street. Behind them came two more motorcycles, side by side. And behind them came a great, open black car, with one Secret Service man walking on the left and one walking on the right side.

Everyone said, "The President!"

The President was waving to the people on the right and to the people on the left. He had two aides, one sitting beside him and one sitting in back of him. They all drove past.

Behind them came two motorcycles, side by side. Then two more motorcycles went by, one on the right and one on the left side of the street. Then came the last motorcycle, all by itself.

When the last motorcycle had gone past, Jacob said, "More."

"All gone," said his father. "Anyway, it's lunchtime."

"**MORE!**" said Jacob.

"**DON'T YELL,**" said his father. "There is no more. The parade's gone, Jacob!"

"**COME BACK!**" yelled Jacob.

"Okay, Jacob," said his father. "It's time you learned you can *not* always have what you want. Call them back. Go on. Yell!"

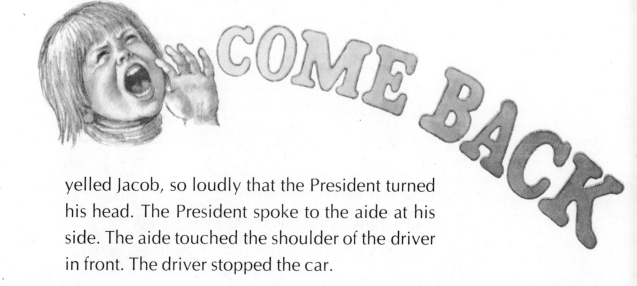

yelled Jacob, so loudly that the President turned his head. The President spoke to the aide at his side. The aide touched the shoulder of the driver in front. The driver stopped the car.

Then the two Secret Service men stopped. The motorcycles in back stopped. One Secret Service man ran forward to stop the motorcycles in front. The men riding those motorcycles hadn't noticed that all the others had stopped.

The President got out of the car and so did the two aides. They came over.

"Did you call me?" asked the President.

"*He* did," said Mitzi. "He's my brother. His name is Jacob."

"Jacob, eh?" said the President.

"And what's your name?" the President asked Mitzi.

"Mitzi," said Mitzi.

"Hello, Mitzi," said the President.

Mitzi said, "And this is my daddy."

"How do you do, Mr. President!" said Mitzi's father.

"Very well, thank you," said the President. "Were you calling me, Jacob?"

"He meant the parade," Mitzi said. "He wants it to come back. He likes parades."

"Likes parades, does he?" said the President.

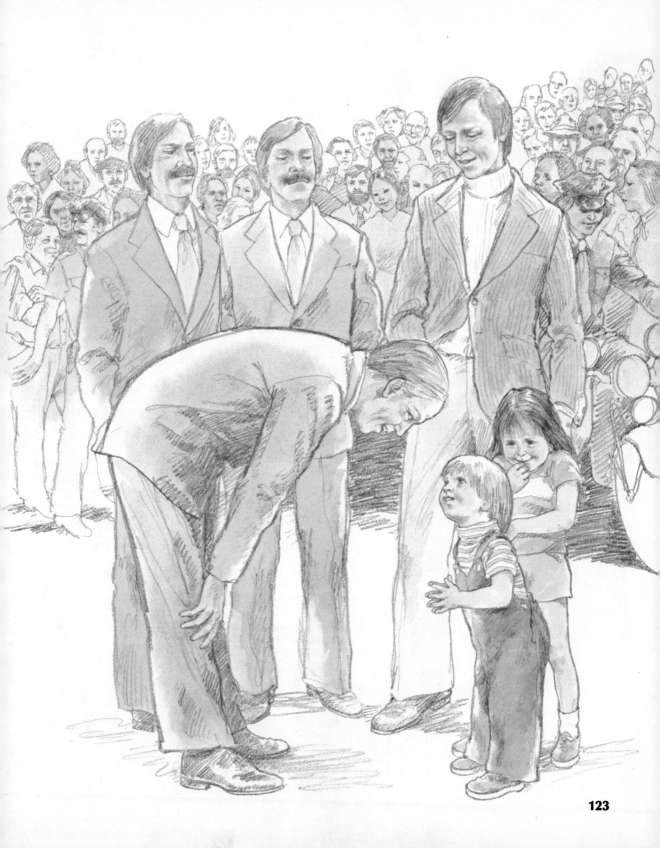

The President turned to his two aides. "Is there any reason why we should be going in that direction rather than in this direction?" he asked.

"One moment, sir," said one of the aides. He ran over to talk to the two Secret Service men. When he ran back he said, "There's no reason, sir, why we should be going in either direction."

"Very well, then," said the President. He turned to Mitzi. "I suppose you like chewing gum," he said.

"Yes, please, and so does Jacob," Mitzi said.

The President looked in his five pockets. "Do either of you happen to have any gum?" he asked the two aides.

The two aides looked in their ten pockets. The Secret Service men looked in *their* ten pockets. The men who rode the motorcycles looked in their fifty pockets. All the people on the sidewalk looked in all of their pockets.

"Great, sir," said one of the aides. "Seventy-five pockets in the President's party alone, and no gum."

"Here's some gum, Mr. President!" somebody yelled.

The driver of the President's car had found a piece of gum in his left trouser pocket. He handed it to one of the Secret Service men. The Secret Service man handed it to one of the two aides. He handed it to the President. The President broke it in half. He gave one piece to Mitzi and the other piece to Jacob.

"Say thank you, Jacob," Mitzi said.

"Well, I won't say goodbye," said the President. "I'll see you when I drive past again."

The President and the two aides walked back to the President's car and got in. The first motorcycle made a U turn. It was followed by the two motorcycles on either side of the street. They were followed by the two motorcycles side by side. Then came the President's car.

"Goodbye!" called the President. He waved as he drove by.

"Goodbye!" cried Mitzi.

"Goodbye," yelled Jacob.

Mitzi and Jacob and their father waved to the President. They waved to the two aides and to the right and the left Secret Service men. They waved to the two motorcycles side by side. They waved to the motorcycle on the right side of the street and to the one on the left. And they waved to the last motorcycle riding by itself. When it had passed, Jacob said, "All gone."

Reflections

1. Could this story really happen? Why or why not?
2. Why were Secret Service men with the President?
3. Why did Jacob yell, "Come back"?
4. How would you feel if you met the President? Why?
5. What famous person would you like to meet? Why? Write three questions you would ask this person.

Wind last night...

Wind last night blew down
A gardenful of peach blossoms.
A boy with a broom
Is starting to sweep them up.

Fallen flowers are flowers still;
Don't brush them away.

— Anonymous

127

The Emperor's New Clothes

Hans Christian Andersen

A long time ago there lived an Emperor. The Emperor liked new clothes. He spent all his time and all his money on clothes.

He did not care about his soldiers or his people. He only left his castle to show off his beautiful new clothes. He had a different suit for each hour of the day.

One day two men came to the court. They called themselves weavers. But they were in fact clever crooks. They pretended that they knew how to weave cloth of the most beautiful colors and patterns. They said the clothes woven from this cloth were magical. Such clothes, they said, would be invisible to anyone who was unfit for the office he held.

"These must be splendid clothes!" thought the Emperor. "I wish I had a suit made of this magic cloth. Then I could find out at once which men in my kingdom are not good enough for the offices they hold. And I should be able to tell who are wise and who are foolish. This cloth must be woven for me right away."

The king ordered that the weavers should be given some gold. "Have them begin their work at once," he said.

So the two men set up two looms. They pretended to be working very hard, though they really did nothing at all. They asked for the most beautiful silk and the best gold thread. This they kept for themselves. And then they went on with their work at the empty looms until far into the night.

Time passed. At last the Emperor said to himself, "I should like to know how the weavers are getting along with my cloth. I am a bit worried about looking at the cloth myself. They said it would be invisible to a fool or a man unfit for his office. I am sure that I am quite safe. But all the same, I think it best to send someone else first."

All the people in the kingdom had heard of the magic cloth. They couldn't wait to learn how wise or foolish their friends and neighbors might be.

"I will send my old Minister to see how the weavers are getting on with my cloth," said the Emperor. "He will be the best one to see how the cloth looks, for he is a wise man. No one can be more fit for his office than he is."

So the old Minister went into the hall to see the cloth. The weavers were working at the empty looms.

"What is this?" thought the old man. He opened his eyes very wide. "I cannot see any thread on the looms. And I don't see any cloth!"

However, he did not speak his thoughts out loud. The men who were pretending to weave asked him to come closer. They pointed to the empty looms. They asked him if he liked the design and the colors.

The poor old Minister could not see anything on the looms. There was nothing there. But, of course, he did not know this. He thought only that he must be a foolish man or unfit for the office of Minister.

"Dear me," he said to himself. "I must never tell anyone that I could not see the cloth."

"Well, Minister," said one of the weavers, "does the cloth please you?"

"Oh! It is most beautiful!" said the Minister quickly. **"The pattern and the colors! I will tell the Emperor how wonderful I think they are."**

The Emperor was pleased by what the Minister told him about the cloth. Soon after, he sent an officer of his court to find out how soon the cloth would be ready.

It was, of course, just the same with the officer as it had been with the Minister. He looked at the looms but could see nothing but empty frames.

"Doesn't the cloth seem as beautiful to you as it did to the Minister?" asked the men. They pointed to the empty looms and talked of the design and colors that were not there.

"It must be that I am unfit for the office I have," thought the officer. "Still, no one need ever know about it."

He turned to the weavers. He said he was happy with the colors and the patterns. "The cloth is magnificent," he later told the Emperor.

The whole city was talking about the splendid cloth which the Emperor had ordered to be woven for so much money.

And now at last the Emperor wished to see the cloth while it was still on the looms. He took with him a few of the officers of the court.

The weavers heard that the Emperor was coming. They pretended to work harder than ever. But they still did not weave one thread through the empty looms.

"Isn't the cloth magnificent?" said the officer and the Minister. "What a splendid design! And what colors!" At the same time they pointed to the empty frames. They thought that everyone else could see the wonderful work of the weavers. But they could not see it themselves.

"How is this?" said the Emperor to himself. "I can see nothing! Am I unfit to be Emperor? That would be horrible!"

Then he cried out loud, **"Oh! The cloth is beautiful. I am so happy with it."**

The officers could see no more than the Emperor. But they all shouted, **"Oh, how magnificent!"** They told the Emperor to have new clothes made from this splendid cloth. They told him to wear the new clothes in the great procession that was soon to take place.

The Emperor pretended to share in the pleasure of his officers. He gave each of the weavers a medal.

Then it was the night before the great procession. The two men had their lights burning all night long. They wanted everyone to see how hard they were working to finish the Emperor's new clothes.

At last they cried, "The Emperor's new suit is ready!"

And now the Emperor and all his court came to see the weavers' work.

"If you will take off your clothes, Emperor, we will fit the new suit in front of the mirror," said the weavers.

The Emperor was then undressed, and the weavers pretended to dress him in his new clothes. The Emperor turned from side to side in front of the mirror.

"How splendid the Emperor looks in his new clothes! And how well they fit!" everyone cried out. **"What a design! What colors!"**

"I am quite ready," said the Emperor. "Do my clothes fit well?" he asked, looking at himself again in the mirror.

"Oh, yes," cried his officers.

The Emperor walked in the middle of the procession right through the streets of the city. All the people cried out, "How beautiful are our Emperor's new clothes!"

In fact, no one would say that he could not see the Emperor's new clothes for fear he would be called unfit for his office.

"But the Emperor has nothing on at all!" said a little child.

"What the child says is true," said the father.

And so it was that what the child said was whispered from one to another. And they all cried out together, "BUT HE HAS NOTHING ON AT ALL!"

The Emperor felt very silly, for he knew that the people were right. But he thought, "The procession has started, and it must go on now!"

So the officers held their heads higher than ever. And they took great trouble to pretend to hold up the coat of the suit which wasn't there at all.

Reflections

1. What do we call this kind of story?
2. What did the emperor care about most of all?
3. Why did the Minister tell the Emperor the cloth was beautiful?
4. What would you have told the Emperor if you were the Minister?
5. What would you have done if you were the Emperor and realized you had nothing on?
6. Imagine that you are watching the procession. Write what you see and feel as the Emperor comes into view.

THE ROYAL TAILOR

The tailor who dresses the King
Has bells on his fingers and bells on his toes,
Bells on his ankles and bells up his nose,
Bells on his kneecaps, hanging by string,
So (if you are wanting some clothes)
Why don't you give him a ring?

(He'll always be at home.)

—*Peter Wesley–Smith*

Hans Christian Andersen

Eva Moore

PART ONE

Hans Wants to Be an Actor

Once upon a time there lived a boy named
Hans Christian Andersen. He was the son of a
shoemaker. Hans lived in the town of Odense in
Denmark.

Hans's mother and father were poor. But
they did all they could to make him happy.

Hans's father did not have money to buy toys
for his son. So he made the toys himself. The
best toy of all was a puppet theater. Hans never
grew tired of watching the puppets.

"When you are bigger," Hans's father told
him many times, "you can make up your own
plays."

Every day Hans asked his father to put on a
puppet play for him. One day his father said,
"Hans Christian, I have a better idea. How
would you like to come with me to the playhouse? You and I will see a real play in a real
theater!"

Hans had never seen a real play. "Is it like
our plays with the puppets?" he asked.

"Better! Much better!" said the shoemaker.
"You will see."

When Hans and his father came near the Odense Playhouse, Hans's father said, "Look, Hans Christian. There is the theater!"

Hans took his father's hand and pulled him to the door. Inside the playhouse, Hans saw rows and rows of chairs. And someone was sitting in every chair. Hans had never seen so many people together in one place.

Just then, the people in the theater stopped talking, and everyone looked at the stage. The lights went out, and Hans Christian Andersen saw a real play for the first time in his life.

When Hans was six years old, he went to school, but he didn't like it very much. He could hardly wait until school was out to go home to his father and the wonderful puppet theater.

But five years later Hans's life changed. His father died. Hans and his mother were alone.

Two years later Hans's mother married again. The family moved into a small house near the river. They were still very poor.

Hans liked to stand in the small garden outside his house and sing. The people who lived nearby would come out to hear him. Sometimes they would ask Hans to come into their homes and sing for them. Hans also acted out plays that he wrote himself.

To Hans there was nothing more wonderful than singing and acting. He made up his mind to become a famous actor.

No one thought Hans could ever be an actor on the stage. His face was too ugly, and he looked clumsy when he walked. It would be better if he learned a trade, people thought.

"Learn a trade," Hans heard from everyone he knew — all but his friend the Colonel.

"Go to high school," said the Colonel. "Then you will be able to make a good living all your life." But the Colonel knew that high school cost a lot of money. He knew that a poor boy like Hans could not go unless someone had the money to send him.

"I will take you to the Odense castle to see Prince Christian," the Colonel told Hans. "Tell the Prince that you want to go to high school. Maybe he will be able to help you."

The Colonel took Hans to the castle. Hans sang a song for the Prince. Then he acted out part of a play. When he had finished, the Prince said, "Well, Hans Christian Andersen, you know how to sing and act. But tell me, what else do you know? What do you want to do?"

Hans knew he should tell the Prince that he wanted to go to school. But he couldn't say it. He had to say what he really felt.

"I want to be an actor in the theater!" he said.

The Prince was very surprised.

"A boy like you would not have much luck in the theater. You should learn a trade," said the Prince.

But Hans wanted to be an actor. And no one—not even the Prince of Odense—could make him change his mind.

One day some actors from the Royal Theater in the city of Copenhagen came to Odense. Hans made friends with the actors. He told them how much he wanted to become an actor. And so to make him happy, they gave Hans a small part in a play they were putting on. Hans knew then that he must go to Copenhagen and get a job in the Royal Theater if he wanted to become a famous actor.

But Hans's mother did not want to let him go. He was so young. What would happen to him in the big city all alone? At last, she took Hans to the old wise woman in Odense. It was said the old woman could see what was going to happen. Maybe she could see what was going to happen to Hans.

The old woman put some cards on the table. She looked at the row of cards and said to Hans's mother, "Your son will become a great man. The world will love him. One day the town of Odense will pay him a great honor."

Hans's mother believed the wise woman. She would not stop Hans. A few days later, Hans left his home and went to Copenhagen.

PART TWO

Hans Becomes Famous

As soon as Hans got to Copenhagen, he went to the Royal Theater to see the manager. But the manager of the Royal Theater had no job for such a strange-looking boy.

"What am I to do now?" Hans thought. "I cannot go back to Odense. I am not yet famous."

Suddenly Hans had an idea. He remembered a famous man he had read about in the newspaper. The man's name was Siboni. He was the head of a big music school in Copenhagen. Maybe Siboni would help him get a job in the Royal Theater.

Hans went to see Siboni and asked to sing for him. At the end of the song, Siboni said to Hans, "You will be a great singer someday."

Siboni and his friends wanted to help Hans. They gave him free singing lessons for a few months. Then Hans's voice changed. The singing lessons stopped.

Hans took acting lessons next. He tried very hard. But his teacher was sure Hans would never be able to act in the theater. So Hans stopped taking acting lessons.

After that, Hans took dancing lessons. His teacher could see that Hans loved to dance. But Hans looked so silly. His teacher knew he would never get a job as a dancer.

Almost three years had gone by since Hans came to Copenhagen to become a famous actor. He was not an actor yet. He was not famous. He did not even have a job.

Hans's biggest worry was money. He had to live on the money his friends gave him. He used most of it to pay for his room. He never had enough warm clothes to wear.

Hans tried to forget his troubles. He made a puppet theater and put on puppet shows for his friends' children. He told the children stories, too. Some stories he had heard when he was a child. Others he made up himself. He was a good storyteller. He pretended to put on a play when he told a story. He would act it all out. Even though the story was make-believe, he made it seem real.

When Hans was alone in his room, he liked to read and write. He wrote plays and put them on in his puppet theater.

Hans sent one of his plays to the directors of the Royal Theater. The directors thought the play was good, but not good enough to be put on in the Royal Theater. "You should go back to school and learn more about writing," one director told Hans. "If you are willing, we will send you to high school. We will pay for everything. Do you want to go?"

"Yes," Hans said to the director, "I would like to go to school."

"Maybe I was born to be a famous writer," thought Hans.

Hans stayed in school until he was twenty-three years old. Then he started to write stories and plays.

After four years of writing, Hans was not rich or famous. But he was making enough money to take trips to other countries.

After one of his trips, Hans came back to Copenhagen and wrote a book called *Life in Italy*. It was sold all over the world. Hans was getting to be famous at last!

The next book Hans wrote was called *Fairy Tales Told for Children*. He had always liked to tell stories to children. Now that he was a writer, he would write them.

Some of Hans's friends thought his fairy tales were the best things he had written. One friend said, "Your book *Life in Italy* will make you famous, Hans. But people will remember your fairy tales."

Hans didn't think his fairy tales were as good as his other books. Still he liked to write them. One story that he wrote was "The Emperor's New Clothes."

By the time Hans was an old man, he was famous. He was famous all over the world. People loved his stories.

The people of Odense had a celebration in honor of Hans Christian Andersen. They wanted to thank him for all the wonderful stories he had given to the world. They were proud that he had been born in their city.

The celebration lasted a week. The mayor of Odense gave a speech about the famous writer. The schools were closed. The children took part in the celebration. At the City Hall, Hans Christian Andersen read one of his stories to the children of the town.

Hans thought about when he was a child. He remembered what the wise woman had told his mother. "Your son will become a great man," she had said. "The world will love him. One day the town of Odense will pay him great honor."

Hans's heart was filled with joy. It had all come true.

Reflections

1. Why did Hans's father make Hans's toys?
2. What did Prince Christian tell Hans?
3. Do you believe that the old wise woman could tell what was going to happen? Why or why not?
4. Why did Hans's singing lessons stop?
5. Who helped Hans decide to go to high school?
6. Why did Hans Christian Andersen become famous?
7. Hans wanted to be an actor. Write a few sentences telling what you would like to be and why.

Statue of Hans Christian Andersen, Central Park, New York City

TALE-SPINNER:
Diane Wolkstein

Diane Wolkstein moans and groans and laughs and cries and shouts and whispers as she spins a tale. And soon the audience is captivated by the wonder and the rhythm of her ageless stories.

For years, Ms. Wolkstein has been New York City's official storyteller. She has regularly told stories in front of the Central Park statue of Hans Christian Andersen. Adults and children alike have enjoyed her performances. Queen Margrethe II and Princess Benedikte of Denmark are among the special visitors who have been enchanted by Ms. Wolkstein's storytelling.

Ms. Wolkstein only tells stories she loves. Two of her special favorites are Hans Christian Andersen's "The Nightingale" and "The Emperor's New Clothes." She believes that a story has many layers, like an onion—a layer for that person, a layer for this time around, and a layer for the next time around.

As a professional storyteller, Ms. Wolkstein tours parks, schools, and libraries across the country, telling stories to people of all ages. She has recorded children's stories and has had her own children's radio program. Ms. Wolkstein has also written children's books and compiled songs for her stories.

ATU, the Silent One

Frank Jupo

PART ONE

Atu and His People

To this day nobody knows where Atu's people came from.

One morning, long ago, they had come out of the desert and had made the African highlands their hunting grounds.

They carried nothing but spears and bows and arrows and a few simple tools. They did not build huts to live in, and they did not till the land to farm.

They called themselves Bushmen.

The Bushmen were always on the move, following wild game. They lived in rocky caves and hunted when they were hungry and needed food.

Living in the highlands was dangerous. Wild animals were never far away from the Bushmen. But at night in their caves they felt safe—safe from wild animals and rain and cold and hot sun.

At night they could rest by the fire, close their eyes, and sleep without being afraid.

Young Atu liked to sit by the fire when he was tired. He was called the Silent One because he could not talk.

Atu had never learned to talk—not the way the others did. But he could talk with his hands.

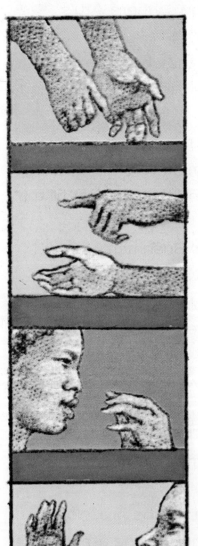

He could do this, and it meant "here."

He could do this, and it meant "there."

If he did this, it meant "hunger."

And if he did this, it meant "thirst."

Atu could say many things in many ways, and his hands hardly ever kept still. He could make his hands talk by making signs. And he could make his hands talk by drawing pictures.

Atu was very good at drawing—drawing things in the sand with his fingers, or on a rock with a piece of burnt firewood.

He could draw trees and birds and animals— all kinds of birds and all kinds of animals.

He could even draw people so that you could guess who they were and what they were doing.

He could draw his mother hunting for honey. He could draw his father making tools.

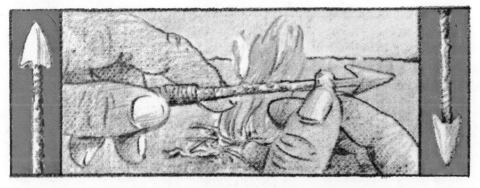

Atu's father was a great hunter, but he was also very good at making tools. From bones and stones and horns and tusks, Atu's father could make a knife or a hammer or a fishhook or an ax.

When the tribe was not hunting, Atu's father sat in front of his cave and worked the long hot day, making the simple tools the people needed.

Sometimes Atu helped him. But most of the time Atu was off and away, playing in the bush or forest.

In the whole wide world there was no place for Atu like the African bush and the forest. There was so much to do. He could take a swim in the water hole, or he could climb trees. He could hide in the grass and watch the wild animals pass nearby on their way to water.

He could follow a giraffe for fun, or keep still and listen as a hungry lion roared far away.

Atu had learned the ways of a hunter. He knew how to move through the bush without being heard or seen. He had learned how to jump and to run. He had learned to find his way through the African bush. He had learned how to throw a spear and how to handle a bow and arrow.

Some of these things Atu learned from playing games. Some he learned listening to the stories told by the brave hunters. "Someday soon I will be a hunter, too," he thought. "I will be brave and hunt dangerous game, so my people will not have to go hungry. Then I, too, will come home with some exciting story, like my father and the other hunters."

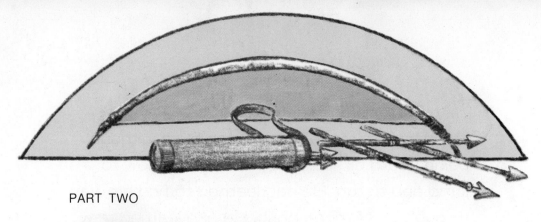

PART TWO

Atu, the Storyteller

One night Atu's people sat around the fire. There was singing and dancing as the headman gave Atu his first full-sized spear and bow and his first poison arrows.

The next morning before the sun was up, Atu's father called him.

"Atu," he said, "the time has come for you to be a hunter."

Atu was on his way with the others. The air was cool, for the sun was still asleep.

The men moved through the bush without a sound, Atu's father in the lead and Atu not far behind. Atu did as the others did as they slipped through the grass across the plain and into the forest.

As the Bushmen stole quietly through the woods, Atu's father suddenly stopped. There in the clearing was the elephant herd—some fanning themselves with their big ears, some just standing in the shade under the trees.

161

But one old bull had caught the smell of the hunters. He raised his trunk over his head and rushed towards Atu. Then he stopped, turned, and hurried away, trumpeting to warn the others. The whole herd took flight. The frightened elephants tore through the bushes and into the open plain.

That was just where the hunters wanted them.

"That one," shouted Atu's father as he pointed at the big bull.

The hunters raced off, parting the bull from the rest of the herd and running him across the bushland.

Holding tight to their bows and spears, they made two lines, with the bull between them. Then spears and arrows flew through the air at the elephant.

The elephant stopped in his tracks and turned around. Trunk raised in anger, ears turned out, he swung his heavy head from side to side.

At that minute one of the hunters jumped toward the elephant and drove his spear right behind his ear. The elephant turned as if to charge. Then he crashed to the ground.
He lay still.

"The big one is dead!" shouted the hunters. Singing and laughing, the men danced around the dead giant. And Atu joined in.

There was great joy when the hunters returned.

"Well done," called the headman. All the people hurried off to collect their part of the kill and then to have a feast.

After the feast, old and young sat together at the meeting place to hear the hunters tell their story.

"There was this great beast," began one hunter. ". . . so I threw my spear," another went on.

Only Atu, the Silent One, was not there to
listen. His father and the headman went to look
for him. They could hardly believe what they
saw when they found him, high up on the side
of a hill.

There, drawn on a rock, the hunt had come
to life! Atu, too, had told his story.

There were the hunters starting out with
their spears and bows. There was Atu himself,
following his father. There were the elephants,
swinging their trunks and fanning with their
ears. There was the great bull elephant, roaring
his rage. And there was Atu's father, ready for
the kill.

"The Silent One has made it so the rock can talk," whispered the headman.

And all through the night Atu's people came in the moonlight to see this new wonder. A story to look at! A story told without words!

As the years passed, Atu became a great hunter like his father and the storyteller of his people.

He told of their world, of the deeds of their hunters, of their games, music-making, and dancing.

He learned to make paint for his pictures from bits of colored earth, and he showed others how to do it, too.

There are some who may say there never really was a boy called Atu, the Silent One. We will never know.

The pictures drawn by the Bushmen have been weathered by the sun and wind and rain. But they can still be seen on the rocks high up near the African desert.

Of Atu's people only a few small tribes are left. But they still hunt on the African plains as of old — the last Bushmen.

Reflections

1. Why don't we know where Atu's people came from?
2. Why did Atu use sign language? What kinds of sign language do we use?
3. Why did Atu's father make tools?
4. Where did Atu get the paint for his pictures?
5. What part of this story is true and what part is make-believe?
6. Do you think there ever was a boy like Atu? Why or why not?
7. Use the pictures on pages 164 and 165 to help you write a description of the hunt.

Talking Without Words

We often tell each other things without using words. We use our hands, our faces, our whole bodies. Look at the pictures below. In which picture is someone saying without words the following:

I love you.
Come here.
I'm mad.
Be quiet.
I'm sleepy.
Hello.

MORNING ARROW

Nanabah Chee Dodge

All summer long Grandmother sat beside her loom. She was weaving a rug out of wool from our sheep. She used her fingers like hidden eyes to feel her way along the rug. Sometimes I sat and watched her weave the colors into a design.

Our home was in the Monument Valley of Utah. Not far distant was Elephant Foot, with its steep sides and flat top. My job was to herd the sheep and goats in the valley. I had to keep them safe from other animals.

One afternoon when the herd was safe, I went to see Grandmother's rug. It was finished, and it was beautiful.

"Morning Arrow, we'll go to the trading post tomorrow," said Grandmother. "We'll sell the rug."

I was ten years old, but this would be my first trip to the trading post. And I would see my first White person.

"Are White people strange, Grandmother?"
I asked.

"They look strange to our eyes," she said,
"but we look strange to theirs. Tomorrow, you
will see your first White friend."

Early next morning we started out on foot for
the trading post. The post was twenty-five
miles away. Grandmother knew the trail from
the days when she could see. She told me to
look for remembered signs. A great rock above,
a waterfall, a spring—all waved us on.

Now and then Grandmother stopped to tie
her shoestrings. "Find me some shoestrings at
the trading post," she said.

Just then I noticed her shawl. It was tattooed
with holes and had lost its bright colors.

As we walked, the rug grew heavier. We
found ourselves resting more often. Once
Grandmother even fell asleep on the soft
grass.

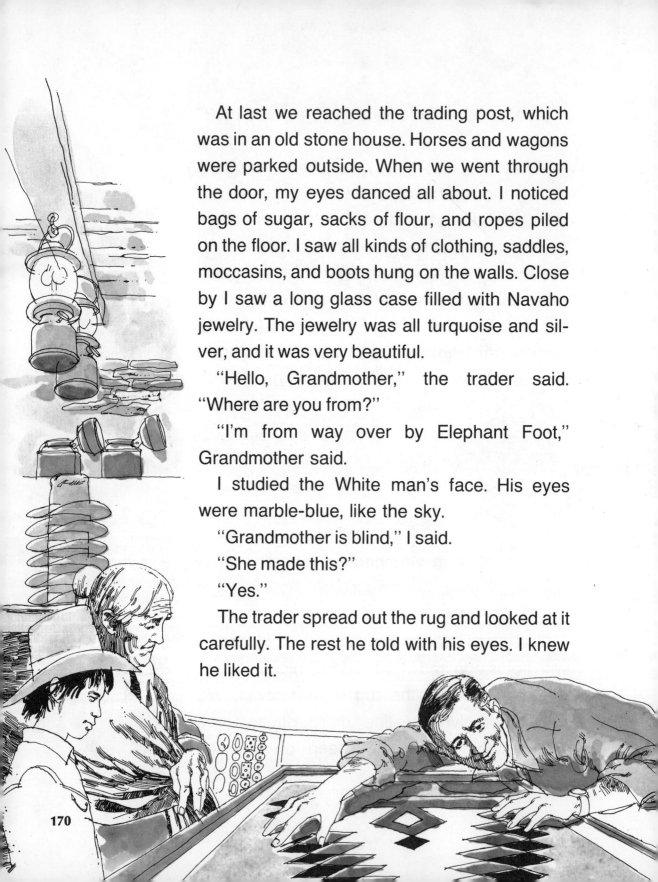

At last we reached the trading post, which was in an old stone house. Horses and wagons were parked outside. When we went through the door, my eyes danced all about. I noticed bags of sugar, sacks of flour, and ropes piled on the floor. I saw all kinds of clothing, saddles, moccasins, and boots hung on the walls. Close by I saw a long glass case filled with Navaho jewelry. The jewelry was all turquoise and silver, and it was very beautiful.

"Hello, Grandmother," the trader said. "Where are you from?"

"I'm from way over by Elephant Foot," Grandmother said.

I studied the White man's face. His eyes were marble-blue, like the sky.

"Grandmother is blind," I said.

"She made this?"

"Yes."

The trader spread out the rug and looked at it carefully. The rest he told with his eyes. I knew he liked it.

"How much?" he asked.

"Is seventy-five dollars too much?" Grand-mother asked the trader.

"No," he said, "Seventy-five dollars seems about right to me." Then he gave Grandmother the money.

With part of the seventy-five dollars Grand-mother bought groceries from the trader. Then she picked up my dusty hat and brushed it off gently. Soon I was dressed in a new hat, boots, a shirt with pants. But Grandmother did not have anything new.

"Grandmother must have something, too," I thought. I looked around the trading post. "How much is that shawl?" I asked. I pointed to one that was hanging on the wall. Its colors were bright turquoise and orange.

"Thirty-five dollars," said the trader.

"I'll be back," I said in a low voice as I picked up Grandmother's groceries.

"All right," the trader said. Both his eyes and his mouth were smiling.

171

Late that fall, Father came for a visit. He had two weeks off from his job, and he wanted to take us to the tribal fair. Proudly I put on a new Navaho costume. "Such a costume goes with one's first trip to the fair," Father said.

Grandmother put on her Navaho costume of green velvet. It was very old, but it was still beautiful. Instead of shoes, she wore moccasins. The moccasins were much softer than her shoes.

It took us three days to reach the tribal fair. People came from all over. Some Navaho sold rugs and turquoise jewelry from their tents. Others sold things that they grew in their gardens.

"Join in the children's races," Father said.

After each race, I came in breathless. My prize money came to sixty cents.

Later, it was exciting to watch the horses and their riders in the ring. And in the evening we watched the many different dances. I remember the music and the singing best.

A few weeks after the fair, the air in the valley turned cold. Winter was near, and I thought more and more about the shawl. One morning, very early, I started out alone for the trading post. Grandmother was still asleep. This time I rode our ram, but he moved slowly. I was tired and hungry when I got to the trading post.

"Well, hello," the trader said. "Where is your Grandmother?"

I made believe I didn't hear his question. "I want to put this money on that shawl," I said. I gave him the sixty cents I had won at the fair. I watched him count the money.

"That's a long way from thirty-five dollars!" he said. "You need far more than this to buy that shawl."

My heart sank. "What do you mean?" I asked.

"I need the price of three lambs," he said. Then he asked me my name.

"Morning Arrow," I said and went outside.

Once outside the trading post I cried quietly. Then I heard the trading post door open.

"Whose ram is that?" called the trader.

"Mine."

"You rode him?"

"Yes."

"You're brave, Morning Arrow," he said. "You're brave to live out there, just you and your grandmother."

Suddenly, I had a brave idea—the ram! "How much would you pay for the ram?" I asked.

The trader looked surprised. "Well, he's young and strong," he said, "and he has good wool." He studied my face. "You'd make a good trader," he said. "All right, I'll trade you the shawl for the ram."

The trader went inside and got the shawl. "Now, how are you going to get home?" he asked.

"Walk," I answered. Then I started out with the shawl.

Getting the shawl was no longer just a dream. Soon I would see Grandmother putting it on. She would love its fresh smell. And I would tell her about its bright colors.

Suddenly a strong wind blew. "Eiyee," I said as the cold went through me. Soon patches of snow began to tattoo the ground. I stood close to a tree and held tightly to the shawl. Nothing must happen to it. Then I thought of Grandmother and of how I left home without telling her where I was going.

Thoughts rushed at me like the falling snowflakes. "Why did I trade the ram for the shawl? Well, Grandmother needed a new shawl. But the ram was part of my father's herd. I should not have traded him for the shawl." I felt big with words. In the end, I knew I must go back to the trading post for the ram.

For a long time I fought the snow and the wind. I felt my way as Grandmother does when she walks alone. Suddenly, I fell down. My eyes closed, but I still held tightly to the shawl.

I was awakened by someone shaking me. "Morning Arrow, Morning Arrow!" a voice called.

"Who is it?" I asked, sitting up.

"Hello, Morning Arrow." It was the trader, whose face I shall never forget.

"Where am I?" I asked.

"About seventy feet from the trading post," he said. "Come in and have something hot to warm you up."

"Where is the turquoise and orange shawl?" I asked.

"It's at your feet," he said. "But your ram ran away. I believe he ran home."

"Did you find me, or did I find you?" I asked.

"I found you," he said. "You were sleeping here in the snow."

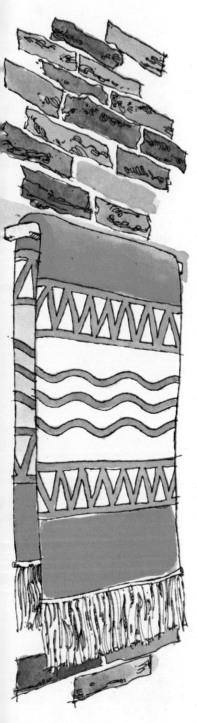

That night I stayed at the trading post. When I awoke I picked up the shawl and made believe it was Grandmother's. Then I began to see things as they really were. I was giving too much thought to a wish, and that was not Navaho teaching. "Sometimes dreams are filled only with pride," Grandmother once said. I quickly dried my tears and put the shawl back on the wall.

Suddenly I remembered that Grandmother wanted new shoestrings. I looked for the shoestrings, found a pair, and left money for them on the counter. Then I started for home.

On the way I heard a noise behind me. It was our ram. We went home together. It was a long slow walk through the snow.

"Hello, Grandmother," I said when I finally reached home.

"That ram ran away, and you went after him?" Grandmother asked quietly.

"No, Grandmother," I said, but she did not seem to hear.

"I was worried, but I knew you would be back," she said.

She wanted to leave it at that, and so did I.

"Oh, I have your shoestrings," I said later.

"Thank you very much," Grandmother said.
I watched her weave the shoestrings through
the small holes in her shoes. I told her that they
were orange like the fruit, and she looked happy.

During the winter, I was away from home
every day, watching the herd. Now the distant
mountains locked arms with the small hills.
Over the top of Elephant Foot, the snow had
placed a white crown. In the valley, only the
jackrabbit painted its way over the hard snow.
All other wild things were gone or hidden away.
It seemed so empty, this world about me.

One day as I was coming home, I heard a
noise. It sounded like a truck on the road.

"Grandmother, was that the trader?" I yelled.

"Yes, my child." I saw her placing the turquoise and orange shawl over her head. "The trader told me he had sold my rug for more than he thought he would get," she said. "So he gave this shawl to me. I feel rich." Her eyes held tears.

I chased after the truck, calling, "Wait, wait!" My arms were flapping like wings. I was breathless.

The truck stopped. I ran to the truck door.

"Thank you," I said to the trader, as I shook his hand and smiled.

The trader took off his glasses. "Here, these glasses are for you," he said. "Merry Christmas, Morning Arrow."

I took the glasses. He watched me put them on. Everything around me turned a dark green. "How beautiful!" I said. "They are mine?"

"Yes, and you look good in them," he said.

We shook hands again and said good-by. I watched the trader drive off before I ran back to Grandmother. She was standing with her shawl wrapped around her. I told her about my new glasses.

"Take me for a walk in my new shawl, Morning Arrow," she said, and we both smiled.

We walked down the road where the truck had gone. Grandmother's hand touched my glasses.

How does the world look to you now?" she asked.

"Beautiful," I said. "Very, very beautiful!"

Reflections

1. What was Morning Arrow's job?
2. Why did Morning Arrow want to buy the shawl?
3. What did Morning Arrow remember best about the fair? What do you like best about fairs?
4. Why did the trader think Morning Arrow was brave?
5. What did Morning Arrow think Grandmother would love about the shawl?
6. Why did Morning Arrow think the world was beautiful at the end of the story?
7. Write a story about a time when the world was beautiful for you.

181

3 ARTISTS AND PERFORMERS

If I were a magician
And in a position
To make dolls dance and hop,

I would also be able
To turn from the table
And make the dancers stop.

—*Lene Hille-Brandts*

183

184

The Great Houdini

Dina Anastasio

On a bright afternoon in the fall of 1905, a small boat pulled away from New York City and headed toward the ocean.

Harry Houdini, the greatest magician in the world, stood alone at the back of the boat watching the waves roll under it. Houdini loved the sea. And yet he also feared it. Each time he had been dropped into the cold ocean with his hands and feet bound tightly, he had feared the sea. Until he had set himself free and was safely back on board the boat, the sea was a dangerous enemy.

In the front of the boat, newspapermen whispered quietly of the important contest they had come to write about.

"He looks tired," a young man said, looking at Houdini, who stood at the other end of the boat. "Put him next to his young student, and I'd say he looks a little old for such dangerous tricks."

"Boudini just might beat that great teacher of his," someone else said.

But most of the crowd just laughed, for they knew only too well that no one was faster than the Great Houdini.

Toward late afternoon, the small boat came to a full stop. While newspapermen watched, the two magicians were searched to make sure that no keys were hidden on them. No one was surprised when nothing was found on either man. Houdini's hands and feet

were then tightly bound with handcuffs and chains. A rope was tied about his middle, in case the men on board had to pull him from the ocean. Then Houdini was helped to the side of the boat. Boudini followed, his feet and hands bound tightly and his life-line in place. Everyone was ready for the contest to begin.

With shouts of good luck from the people on the boat, Houdini and his student were dropped into the cold ocean. The first

one to free himself would win the contest and be known as the greatest magician in the world. Would it be Houdini or Boudini?

The newspapermen stood along the side of the boat, waiting silently for a sign of life from the water below.

"One minute," someone called. The men searched the waves carefully. But there was no sign of Houdini or his student.

"It looks mighty cold down there," one man said quietly.

"Bet it feels even colder," said another.

"One minute, thirty seconds," a voice shouted from the back of the boat. Still, there was no sign of life from the ocean below.

Then suddenly a man bobbed up from the deep. He waved his hands so that all could see that they were free of handcuffs and chains. It was the Great Houdini!

"Boudini up yet?" he called.

"Not yet," someone answered.

Houdini smiled and ducked back under the water to free his feet from the handcuffs and chains.

Once more, the newspapermen searched the dark ocean for signs of life.

"Where's Boudini?" one of them asked.

"I don't know, but it looks like Houdini has done it again," another man answered.

In a minute Houdini bobbed up again. He was short of breath but still smiling. His feet were free from the handcuffs.

"Is Boudini up yet?" he asked, and was pleased to hear that his student had not yet been seen. Again, Houdini ducked under the water. Now he had only to free his feet from the chains.

When Boudini still failed to come up, the crowd on board the bobbing boat began to worry. They stood silently and searched the dark water for some sign of life. A head was soon seen, but it was Houdini again.

"Is he up yet?" he called. But this time, when someone shouted no, the magician didn't smile. Now he, too, was worried.

Slowly he swam to the boat and pulled himself on board. In one hand he carried his handcuffs and chains. Someone handed him a quilt, and he hugged it about himself and went to the side to wait with the others.

"You'd better pull him out," Houdini said.

Soon Boudini was being lifted gently on board by the rope around his middle. His hands and feet were still in chains. His lips were blue from the cold. He was fighting to get his breath.

When he was able to speak, he looked up at Houdini, who waited beside him, and whispered,

"I swallowed some water."

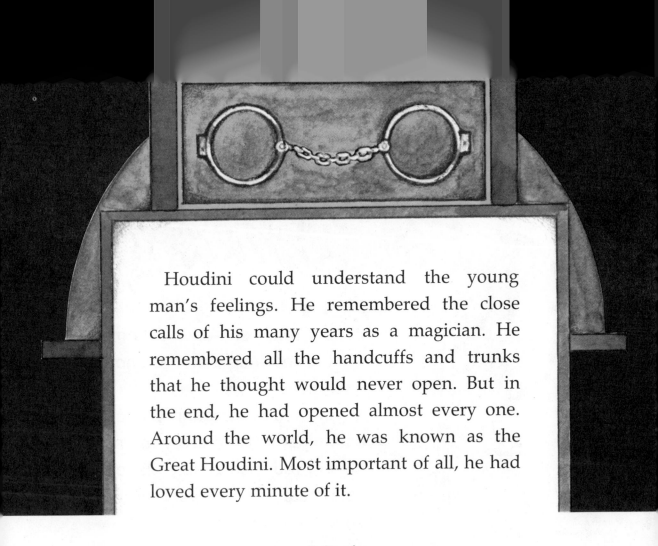

Houdini could understand the young man's feelings. He remembered the close calls of his many years as a magician. He remembered all the handcuffs and trunks that he thought would never open. But in the end, he had opened almost every one. Around the world, he was known as the Great Houdini. Most important of all, he had loved every minute of it.

Reflections

1. What did this contest show the world about Houdini?
2. How was age an advantage to Boudini or Houdini in this contest?
3. Do you think this contest should have been held in the fall? Why or why not?
4. What do you think happened to Boudini after he was dropped into the ocean?
5. Why was Houdini known as a great magician?
6. Make a list of the things Houdini did from the first time he bobbed up to the point when he pulled himself onto the boat.

Stretching Sentences

Read the sentences below. Which one tells the most?

1. My dog eats.
2. My big red Irish setter eats meat.
3. My big red Irish setter, Clancy, eats meat happily.
4. My big red Irish setter, Clancy, eats meat happily every morning.
5. My big red Irish setter, Clancy, eats meat happily every morning on our back steps.

Now you take a turn. Write sentences about a pet you would like to have.

1. First tell what your pet plays.
2. Then add what your pet is.
3. Then add your pet's name.
4. Then add when he plays.
5. Then add where he plays.

Artists and Performers

Egyptian Harpist

ARTIST UNKNOWN

Entertainment and performers have long been favorite subjects among artists. This Egyptian wall painting of a young musician singing for a man and his wife is well over three thousand years old. The young man is playing the harp, our oldest string instrument. The harp was once as popular among singers as is the guitar today.

PHOTOGRAPH, ERICH LESSING, MAGNUM

(detail)

Family of Saltimbanques

PABLO PICASSO (pi kä ´sō), 1881–1973

Pablo Piscasso has painted many pictures of circus performers. The one on the left shows a circus family between performances. Can you tell what each person does in the circus? Do the performers seem as happy and full of fun as you might expect?

The Actors Iwai Hanshirô IV and Sawamura Sôjûrô III

TORII KIYONAGA (kē yō nä gä), 1752–1815

The picture below of the two Japanese actors was printed in color on a wood-block. Notice how the shapes and colors give us a feeling of peace and harmony.

TOKYO NATIONAL MUSEUM

195

Oscar Pettiford

DENNIS STOCK, 1928–

There are many different kinds of artists.
Dennis Stock is a well-known photographer
of jazz musicians. Below is his photograph
of Oscar Pettiford, a great bass player. In it,
the musician's sensitive face and hands seem
to frame the top part of his instrument.

Mabel Godwin

JILL FREEDMAN

This is a photograph by Jill Freedman of jazz pianist Mabel Godwin. By capturing the performer's emotional intensity at the piano, the photographer lets us share the player's feelings. The photographer also makes use of reflection to show another perspective of the pianist in action.

Greek Harpist or Singer

ARTIST UNKNOWN

In ancient Greece, as in ancient Egypt, actors and singers played the harp as they spoke or sang their lines. Here is a bronze statue of a Greek musician playing the harp, which the Greeks called a lyre.

IRAKLION ARCHEOLOGICAL MUSEUM, CRETE
PHOTOGRAPH. ERICH LESSING, MAGNUM

197

THE LOUVRE, PARIS

198

Performance of "La Contessa dei Numi"

GIOVANNI PAOLO PANNINI (pä nē´nē), 1692–1765

Few entertainments are as colorful and exciting as an opera or ballet staged with beautiful scenery and costumes for an audience, itself beautifully dressed. Pannini caught this spirit in this painting of an opera performance in honor of the birth of a French prince.

The Dancer

EDGAR DEGAS (dā gä´), 1834–1917

The French painter Degas is famous for his paintings of ballet dancers on and off stage. His use of color gives us a sense of movement and a feeling of joy.

THE LOUVRE, PARIS (ZIOLO)

199

Snowing

MARC CHAGALL (shə gäl'), 1887 –

In his paintings, Marc Chagall often puts in char-
acters from the folktales he heard in Russia as a boy.
This painting has a make-believe quality.

The Acrobats

Flying high on silver bars
Ladies spangled like the sun
Turn just so, and then let go—
and catch one another!
And smile when they come down, and wave,
And are not proud of being brave.

—Dorothy Aldis

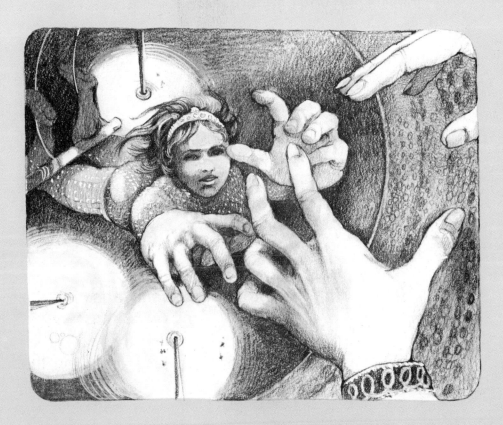

Magic Secrets

Rose Wyler and Gerald Ames

Here are some magic tricks for you. Practice the tricks before a mirror to see how they look. All magicians do this. Talk while you do each trick. While you're talking, you can make your friends laugh and make them think what you want them to think. Then you can fool them.

Write Through Your Hand

Say, *"I will write through my hand. First I make a mark here."*

Mark your palm with ink, and close your hand while the ink is wet. Then mark the back of your hand.

Say, *"Mark, go through my hand and make a cross on my palm."*

Open your hand, and there is a cross on the palm of your hand!

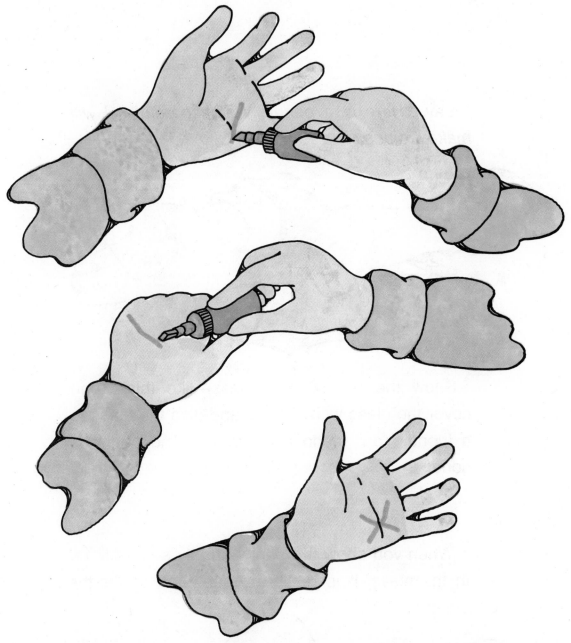

The secret:

If you put the first mark in the right place, it makes a cross when you close your hand.

Good-by, Penny

Say, *"Here is a penny. Watch carefully. I will make it disappear."*

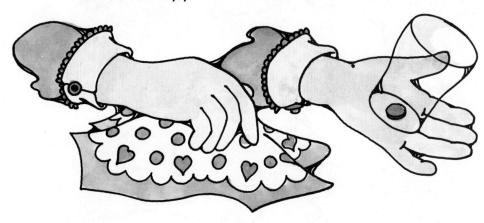

Show the penny in a glass—like this. Then cover the glass with a cloth, and give the glass to a friend. Your friend looks into it. The penny is gone!

The secret:

When you show the penny, it only *seems* to be in the glass. It is really in your hand *under* the glass.

Bag of Surprises

Show a paper bag and say, *"It is empty."*

Then reach into the bag and pull out a present for everybody—ribbons, pictures, a handkerchief.

The secret:

There are really two bags, one inside the other. The inside bag is empty. The presents are under it in the other bag.

Push a Glass Through a Table

Set a plastic glass on the table. Take a piece of newspaper and press the paper around the glass. Hold up the paper to show the glass is still inside.

Say, *"I use paper so I won't hurt my hand if the glass breaks. Now I'll put the glass back on the table."*

Then push down on the paper. Push and push until—**bang!** The glass hits the floor. But does it really go through the table?

The secret:

After showing the glass in the paper, let the glass slip into your lap. Only the paper goes on the table. Its shape fools your friends. They think the glass is still under it. As you push down on the paper, let the glass fall from your lap to the floor.

Mystery Marble

Show a marble in your hand. Then cover it with a handkerchief.

Say, *"Feel under the handkerchief. Is the marble still there?"*

All your friends feel the marble. It is still there. You flick away the handkerchief. *The marble is gone!*

The secret:

The last one to feel the marble is your helper. Your helper takes the marble away.

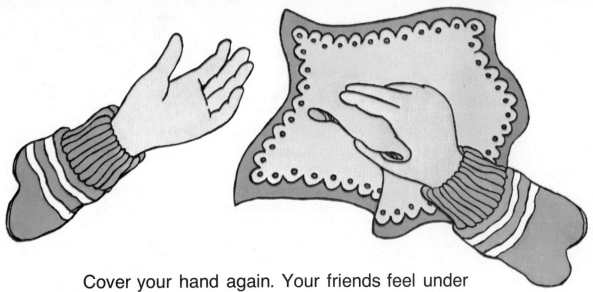

Cover your hand again. Your friends feel under the handkerchief again. The marble is not there. When you lift the handkerchief, the marble is back.

The secret:

This time your helper puts it back.

On Pointe!

The world of ballet is a world of light, music, movement, change. It is a solo dance or a duet. It is the grace and sweep of a ballet corps. It is a story in mime and dance. And it is dance with music, but without a story.

The ballerina and her partner, who take their bows before an admiring audience, have probably lived and worked with ballet since the age of eight or nine. In the beginning they found that learning to dance is not at all like learning to play a game. The five basic ballet positions must be learned slowly until they become natural. The leaps and turns and the light, flowing connecting movements come next. And there is always practice and more practice. Not that ballet steps are hard or painful if they are well-taught. But the student must make a habit of doing them perfectly!

Alicia Alonso rehearsing "Giselle."

Gelsey Kirkland and Mikhail Baryshnikov in "Theme and Variations."

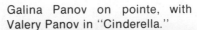

In ballet school, students move ahead as they develop as dancers. If they are very good dancers, most of them will make their stage debut in five or six years. Their goal is to be part of a ballet company and maybe even to be one of its main dancers. Many ballet companies have their own ballet schools. In this way the school and the company are able to work together to keep ballet and its traditions young, fresh, and alive. Together, the school and the company create both the artists and the art.

Cynthia Gregory and Rudolf Nureyev, with the ballet corps in "Swan Lake."

Joe Wyatt, M. Elena Carter, and Susan Lovelle of the Dance Theatre of Harlem in "Concerto."

Galina Panov on pointe, with Valery Panov in "Cinderella."

211

HATTIE, the Backstage Bat

Don Freeman

The backstage of a dark, empty theater is a lonely place where only a bat would feel at home. To a little bat named Hattie, this **was** home.

Hattie had lived in the Grand Theater all her life, so she had never seen a green tree or a haunted house. She had never flown in the bright moonlight the way other bats do.

For Hattie, the sky was the space high above the stage. Every night she flew about for hours at a time, sweeping in and out of the rafters and between the stage curtains.

Then, when she was tired, she landed on a rope, folded her wings tightly against her sides, and hung upside down by her claws to sleep.

The only one who knew about Hattie was Mr. Collins. He came in every morning to clean.

There hadn't been a show in the old Grand Theater for quite a long while, but Mr. Collins was never lonely. He had Hattie. Once he made her a little hat out of things he found in an old trunk.

Each noontime Mr. Collins pulled his chair to the middle of the stage and shared his lunch with his friend. He knew that bats like to eat flowers, so he always brought Hattie daisies.

While they ate, Hattie listened as Mr. Collins talked about the wonderful plays that had been given on this very stage.

One afternoon he had very important news to tell Hattie. "Starting today, some actors are coming here to rehearse a new play," he said. "That means you will have to stay out of sight. I don't know why, but people get very frightened when they see a bat flying around."

Then Mr. Collins began to shoo Hattie into the rafters. "I'm sorry to have to do this, my dear," he shouted, "but it's for your own good as well as mine. We want the play to be a success, don't we?"

So Hattie did as she was told. The actors had no idea a bat hung high above them as they sat reading their parts in the play.

Day after day, the actors came in to rehearse their parts until they knew all their lines by heart. Day after day, Hattie kept well out of sight. It was only late at night that Hattie flew down to the stage and ate the food Mr. Collins had left for her.

One morning Hattie heard the sound of hammering. The set for the play was being built on the stage. Hattie saw, for the first time in her life, not only a tree but a three-story house! It was a haunted house. It even had a tower-attic made to order for a bat!

Weeks went by, and finally there was a dress rehearsal. Hattie watched in surprise as an actor, wearing a long black cape and looking like a huge bat, began to climb in and out of the windows of the house.

"Why doesn't he fly the way I do?" she asked herself. "I could show that actor how to act like a bat." But Hattie didn't dare move from the rafters.

Then, at last, it was opening night. Everyone backstage was worried and excited. But because of Hattie, Mr. Collins was more worried than anyone else. Hattie had been very good, but would she still stay out of sight on this, the most important night of all?

People in beautiful evening clothes entered the theater and took their seats. Since they had come to see a mystery play, they were ready to be scared out of their wits.

The theater lights dimmed, and everyone was silent. Slowly the curtains opened. The actor dressed as a bat entered and stole quietly across the stage.

But the audience had seen plays about batmen many times before. They were not excited about seeing another one.

"I wanted to see a **scary** play," said one lady.

"So did I," whispered another. "Batmen! That's not exciting!"

But high up in the rafters, Hattie was finding the play very exciting. She loved the blue light that filled the stage. "What a night for a bat like me!" thought Hattie. She could hold herself back no longer!

Down she flew, sweeping through the open attic window, across the beam of the bright spotlight, and above the heads of the audience.

As Hattie began to dart in and out of the beam of light, suddenly the audience saw something that made their hair stand on end.

A huge shadow of a bat fell across the whole stage! Men gasped! Ladies screamed! Eyes popped! Everyone was scared stiff.

What an uproar the audience made when they found out that it was a **real** bat sweeping above their heads. The uproar was too much for Hattie. All at once, in plain sight of everyone, she flew back through the attic window and disappeared backstage.

The audience stood and clapped. **"Bravo, bat!"** they shouted. **"Bravo!"**

Hattie had saved the show. The play was a huge success.

Of course, Hattie was asked to do her flying act each night after that. She was a great star, and as you might have guessed, every night after every show Mr. Collins proudly gave Hattie a white rose.

Reflections

1. Would you rather see a movie or a play? Why?
2. Why do actors rehearse a play many times before opening night?
3. Why did Mr. Collins want Hattie to keep out of sight?
4. How did everyone backstage feel on opening night?
5. Why did the audience stand, clap, and shout, "Bravo!" after Hattie disappeared?
6. Write how you would feel and act if you were in the audience when Hattie flew around.

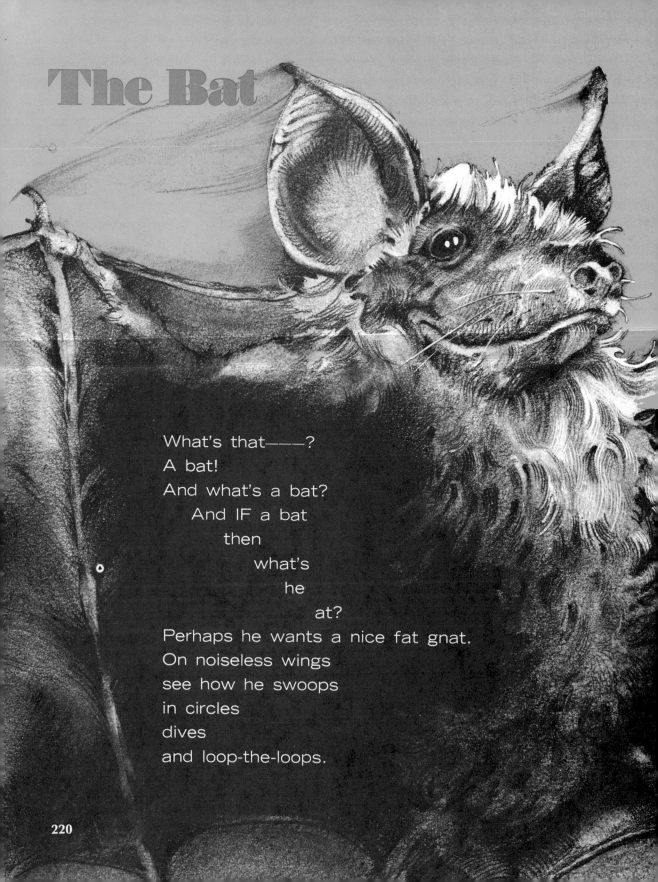

The Bat

What's that——?
A bat!
And what's a bat?
    And IF a bat
        then
            what's
                he
                    at?
Perhaps he wants a nice fat gnat.
On noiseless wings
see how he swoops
in circles
dives
and loop-the-loops.

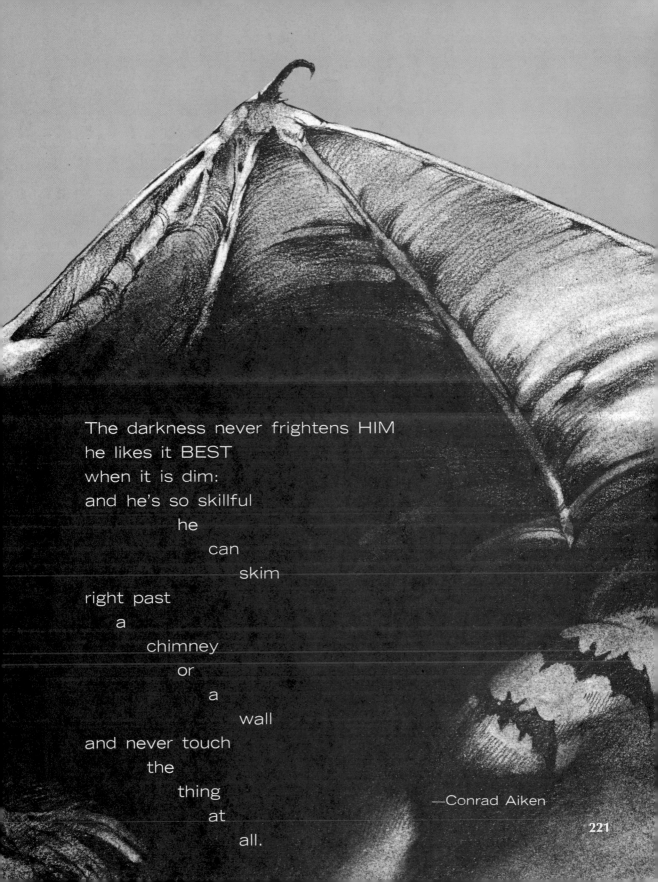

The darkness never frightens HIM
he likes it BEST
when it is dim:
and he's so skillful
    he
        can
           skim
right past
   a
      chimney
       or
         a
           wall
and never touch
   the
      thing
        at
         all.

—Conrad Aiken

221

Rita Golden Gelman

SHIRLEY TEMPLE
The Girl Who Made People Happy

"Arms out. Bend your knees. Back straight. Head high."

Four-year-old Shirley Temple was in dancing school. Her golden curls bounced as she moved her head. Her eyes sparkled. Shirley liked to dance.

When class was over, Shirley and her mother were the first to leave. Mrs. Temple had the car started, ready to go home. Suddenly, the dancing teacher ran out to stop them. A movie scout, who was looking for children to act in the movies, had just come to the school. Shirley and her mother went back in. The movie scout watched as the class paraded in front of him.

About two weeks later, Shirley's mother got a call from some movie people. They wanted Shirley to be in a movie. At first, Shirley's father said no. He didn't want his daughter in movies. She was too young. But then he changed his mind. Shirley was allowed to take her first step toward fame.

Shirley's first movies were very short. And to most people today, they might seem silly. Little children were dressed partly in grown-up clothes and partly in baby clothes. Still, Shirley had fun making the movies and dressing up. The costume she liked best at that time had lots of blue feathers and sparkles. Shirley thought it was "really dreamy."

For two years, Shirley made short movies. Then, in 1934, when she was six years old, she began making long movies. She was a success right away.

When Shirley danced, her golden curls bounced with every step. When she smiled, two dimples popped into her cheeks. And when she sang, her voice carried those who listened into a happy, magical world. Most moviegoers soon fell in love with Shirley Temple. Her films made people forget their troubles.

Back then, in the 1930's, jobs were few. Many people had little money for the things they needed. It was a hard, sad time for the whole country. When they could, people tried to forget their troubles by going to the movies. They wanted to smile. They wanted to feel more cheerful. Shirley Temple helped them to feel happier.

Even famous movie stars had fun when Shirley was around. They played hide-and-seek with her on the movie set. They sat on the ground with her and played jacks. Shirley had so much energy that other people felt more alive when she was there.

Being a movie star was very exciting. Everywhere Shirley went, people waved and called to her. They bought Shirley Temple dolls, Shirley Temple coloring books, and Shirley Temple cutouts. Girls all over the country wore Shirley Temple clothes. They curled their hair in Shirley Temple curls. And they sang Shirley Temple songs. "On the Good Ship Lollipop" was Shirley's most popular song.

Many people who saw Shirley in the movies began to think of her as their own little girl. Shirley received letters from all over the world. She received dolls, too. Shirley received so many dolls that her family had to build a special house just for the dolls.

Because movies were so popular in the 1930's, the companies that made them were very successful. As a result, the movie stars themselves received large sums of money for their acting.

When Shirley made her first movies, she was paid ten dollars a day. But in only a few years, she was earning thousands of dollars every day. By the time she was ten years old, she had made more than five million dollars.

To Shirley, her life in the movies was like a wonderful dream. She was doing what she liked best to do. And she was fast becoming a famous movie star. Most of the time it was fun. But not always.

For one thing, Shirley couldn't go to school with other children. She spent every day at the studio while she was making a movie. Besides, other children became excited when they were near a famous movie star. Sometimes they forgot that Shirley was real. They would touch her. They would even pull her hair. Shirley never knew the fun of learning with other children.

★ ★

Shirley had to have her own teacher. She studied with the teacher in between her work making movies. She had a special room and play yard at the studio. There, she did her schoolwork and played—mostly with grown-ups and animals.

Shirley loved animals. When she was seven, she wrote, "I am going to get my mother to buy me some foxes and chickens for my play yard at the studio. I already have twenty-four rabbits, and that is funny. I started with four that the studio gave me. Then Mother, Dad, and I went away. When I came back, there were twenty little ones. I guess I will have to make the coop very much larger. . . ."

What did Shirley Temple do with the money she made as a child star? All of her movie money went into a bank, all, that is, except four dollars a week. This was given to her as spending money.

"Four dollars isn't enough for all the candy, chewing gum, and soda I need when I work," Shirley wrote in 1935. Shirley always treated the other children who worked with her on the set. And sometimes her spending money didn't go very far.

A growing number of today's boys and girls are also getting to know Shirley Temple the child star. Shirley's movies are often shown on TV. And collecting records of her movie songs is also popular with many young people.

When she grew up, Shirley made only a very few movies. She got married and had three children. Then, when her children were grown, Shirley became interested in government. In 1969, she worked for the United Nations. In 1974, the President of the United States made her Ambassador to Ghana, a country in West Africa.

Shirley later became the State Department Chief of Protocol. She met many important people from other countries. Most of them remembered her as a little girl singing and dancing in movies. Shirley Temple Black, as an adult, helped make their visits to the United States pleasant.

The grown-up Shirley has worked hard to make the world a better place to live in. The child Shirley did that without even trying. Over the years, many people still remember the Shirley Temple who danced and tapped and laughed and sang. They remember the dimples. They remember the golden curls. And they remember the little girl who made them happy.

Reflections

1. In the 1930's, why did people go to the movies whenever they could?
2. Why did girls all over the country want to look like Shirley Temple?
3. How were Shirley Temple's school years different from other children's?
4. Why didn't she often play with children her age?
5. Write a letter to a friend telling what you enjoy about going to school with other children.

★ ★ ★ ★ ★ ★ ★ ★ ★ ★ ★ ★ ★ ★ ★ ★ ★

Suppose I Were a Snowflake

Suppose I were a snowflake
Floating to the ground
Watching all the other flakes
Sailing all around

Suppose I were a bird
Flying in the sky
Making myself a home
In an oak tree, oh so high

Suppose I were an angel
With wings of silver and gold
Then I could get bigger
But never very old

But let's suppose I were myself
Just regular, plain, old me
Then I could suppose and suppose
The things that I could be.

—Trudy Abramchik, age 11

Ann McGovern

If You Lived With the CIRCUS

The man on the flying trapeze turns somer-saults in the air. The woman leaps easily from horse to horse. The lion trainer steps out of the lion cage without a mark on her. A clown falls from a high ladder. He laughs as he gets up.

"It looks so easy," you think.

But if you lived with the circus, you would know that it's not easy. Circus people work hard to make their acts look easy.

Most performers start to practice when they are young. And they have to practice all the time.

Circus performers give two or three shows a day, six days a week.

When they aren't working, they are thinking of new ways to make their acts better for next year. Then they must practice the new acts.

Some people become clowns by going to school. Who are the teachers at the clown school? Other clowns!

For six weeks, five days a week, men and women work hard at being clowns. They learn to walk on stilts, to climb up on an elephant, and to put on clown make-up. They also learn all about famous clowns and the acts they do.

There are three kinds of clowns:
the whiteface clown,
the August clown,
and the acrobat clown.

Whiteface clowns look as if they were about to cry. They wear torn clothes, old shoes and hats, and sad, sad faces.

Nothing that whiteface clowns do in their act turns out right. A whiteface clown picks up a chair, and the chair falls to pieces. A spotlight shines on the floor. The whiteface clown tries to sweep the light away, but it keeps moving away.

August clowns are funny slapstick clowns. August clowns wear pants that fall down, noses that light up, and large shoes that they trip over.

Acrobat clowns do their funny tricks on tightropes or turn somersaults on the backs of horses.

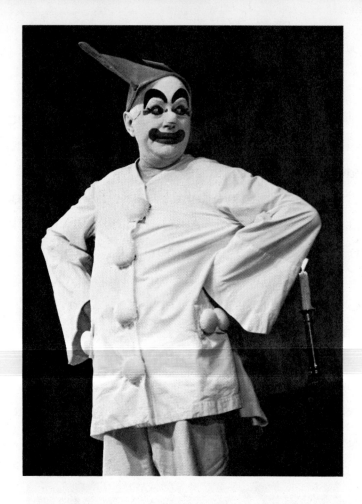

Circus people call small clowns the "little people." These clowns are the midget clowns who are no higher than four feet.

The tall clowns in the circus are sixteen feet tall. That's almost as tall as three grownups. Does that sound impossible? It is.

The tall clowns are ordinary clowns who walk on high stilts. Walking on stilts is dangerous. It takes a lot of practice. If a clown should start to fall, he cannot jump off his stilts. They are tied to his legs, under his clothes.

If you lived with the circus, you would know how the clowns do all their tricks. Here are two clown tricks.

Tiny car trick: A tiny car drives into the circus ring. Suddenly the door opens. A clown comes out—and another and another and another. Ten clowns may come out of the car. How can so many clowns fit into such a tiny car? The secret is that the car is empty inside. It has no engine and no seats. The clowns in the act are good acrobats. They can fold themselves up so that they don't take up much space.

Saw-a-clown-in-half trick: A clown begins to saw another clown in half. The saw goes right through the body of the clown. But suddenly the two halves of the body jump up and run out of the ring. The secret? The two halves are really two midget clowns.

If you lived with the circus, you would know that circus acts are dangerous. Think of two acrobats on the high trapeze. If one should reach for the other in midair and miss, the other acrobat would fall.

A safety net is below the high wires. But it is safe only if you fall into it in the right way. Each performer knows the right way to fall. If he does not fall the right way, he might break some bones.

If you lived with the circus, you would know why the tiger trainer needs chairs in his act. He trains his tigers to keep their eyes on his chair. Then if a tiger should attack, it will attack the chair, not the trainer.

If a tiger gets frightened, it looks for a quiet, dark corner. It will attack only the people who get in its way.

Once a tiger got out of its cage in a circus in New York City. It knocked down a clown and ran toward the lobby. One of the midget clowns thought of all the children standing in the lobby who might get hurt. He bravely jumped in front of the tiger. All he had was a tiny whip which he began waving at the tiger. The tiger was so surprised that it turned around and ran out of the lobby and back into the circus ring. It was captured in a big net and led back to its cage.

Most circus animals don't go far when they run away. One night two circus girls were alone in their tent with their pet dog. The dog suddenly began barking. When the girls looked up to see why the dog was making so much noise, they saw a big brown bear standing at the door of the tent.

The girls grabbed the little dog. They were too frightened to yell. The bear walked all around the tent and then out the door and back to its cage.

If you lived with the circus, you would have lots of surprises!

Circus Talk

"Hey, First-of-May! Tell the butcher in the backyard to stay away from the bulls. We have some cherry pie for him before doors."

Double talk? No, circus talk. The circus world has words all its own. Here are some of them:

First-of-May: Anyone who is new to circus work. It comes from the old days when the circus began its year about the first day of May. New people were hired to set up tents, give water to the elephants, or to work at anything that needed doing.

Butcher: Someone who sells hot dogs and souvenirs to the audience during the show.

Backyard: The place where performers wait before they go into the ring to do their act.

Bull: Any circus elephant, even though most of the elephants are female.

Cherry pie: Extra work. Some people say it was first called "chairy pie." Sometimes performers have to set up extra chairs around the arena for the audience.

Doors!: The cry that tells the circus people that the audience is coming in to take their seats.

Big Top: **Where the circus takes place, the circus arena or tent.**

Clown stop: **A time for the clowns to perform between acts.**

Home run: **The trip from the place where the last show is given back to the circus headquarters.**

Home Sweet Home: **The last show of the year.**

Joey: **What clowns are called—named for Joseph Grimaldi, an actor who joined a circus as a clown about 200 years ago.**

Kinker: **Any circus performer.**

Razorbacks: The people who help set up a circus and take it down again.

Spec: The big parade in the circus in which all performers take part.

Stripes: Tigers.

Walkaround: The parade of all the clowns around the arena.

Web: Long ropes which hang down from the top of the arena. Trapeze performers do tricks on the webs.

Websitters: The people who stand on the ground holding the bottom of the ropes.

4 SPECIAL HAPPENINGS

When Something Happy Happens

When something happy happens,
You think of it now and then,
And it's like a lovely present
That you look at over again.

You untie the silky ribbon
And remove the wrapping with care.
Then you reach down deep inside the box
For the thing that is lying there.

And after you've looked and looked
And looked,
Till you no longer feel the yen,
You put it back in its roomy
Box and gently wrap it again.

—*Marci Ridlon*

Phillip Viereck

Let Me Tell You About My Dad

I never used to think that my dad was anything special. He was just my dad—the man I lived with. There's only been the two of us since Mother died. And that was when I was very little.

Of course, I've always liked my dad. But he always seemed to be kind of ordinary. He worked in a factory. One evening a week he liked to bowl. On weekends he worked in the yard or did other chores. We never did anything really exciting.

Then one day, Dad got a letter from his old friend, Bill, who lived in Alaska. Dad had met Bill in the army. He had worked with him many years ago. In the letter Bill asked Dad to take a long vacation and come to Alaska. He wanted Dad to help him build a log cabin in the woods for hunters and for people who came there on vacation.

Dad and I talked about it. I said I'd sure like to go. He said that maybe we could.

"Do you know how to build a log cabin?" I asked.

"I'm not too bad with an ax," he answered.

I didn't know that he'd ever had an ax in his hands. He'd never talked about it.

The next day at the factory, Dad asked for extra vacation time. He got it, without pay, of course. And on the very afternoon that school was out, we started for Alaska.

Heading north toward Canada, we drove through many miles of flat farmland. Then we came to mountains that were high on the sides and flat on top. I'd never seen mountains like them. We bought our meals in towns along the way. At night we stopped to camp wherever we could find a place by the side of the road.

One day we came to a place where two cars had crashed into each other. People were crying and shouting. Dad stopped to see if anyone was hurt.

There was a man with a broken leg that nobody was doing anything about. Dad made a splint for it.

When we drove away, I said, "You were the only one who knew what to do, Dad."

"I am sure that some of those people knew how to splint a broken leg," he said. "They were just too excited to be of any help."

Our first few days in Canada, we drove through more flat farmland—almost all of it planted in wheat. Then we came to a land of thick forests and big rivers. The towns got farther and farther apart. Finally the last one of any size was behind us. Ahead were 1500 miles of wild country.

The wild country of Canada was beautiful. The road wound up and around steep mountains. There were forests, lakes, and rivers. We cooked our own meals. Sometimes we went fishing, and Dad cooked the fish over a campfire.

At last we got to Fairbanks, Alaska, where Bill lived. There were wide streets and lots of stores and hotels. I was surprised to find such a big city so far north.

Bill was sure glad to see us. His wife, Ellen, cooked us a big meal. It was great after so much of our own cooking.

We spent the next two days getting food, tools, and supplies into a wagon. Bill had a bulldozer that would be able to pull the wagon into places where no truck could go.

Finally we were ready to go. It was some job getting the supplies over hills, through woods, and across streams. We followed a trail that Bill had already marked with flags or by cuts in trees.

Dad drove the bulldozer. Most of the time Bill and I walked because riding in the wagon was so bumpy.

I was surprised that my dad knew how to drive a bulldozer. Bill told me that he had been the best bulldozer driver in the army. He sure drove it into places I thought he'd never get out of.

It doesn't get dark early that far north, so we kept going until late. It was ten o' clock when we got to Mirror Lake, where we were going to build the cabin. We were so tired, we just got into our sleeping bags, clothes and all, and fell asleep.

The next morning when I got up, I saw how beautiful Mirror Lake was. All around it were tall dark evergreens, that you could see in the clear quiet water of the lake. Now and then there was a little wave in the lake, which I guessed had been made by a beaver.

Suddenly, I heard the far-off sound of an airplane. It was Ellen bringing us more supplies.

The four of us worked hard those next few days. We put up tents to live in while we were building the cabin. With the bulldozer, Dad cleared a place for the cabin. He and I brought rocks from the bed of a nearby stream. We used them to build the foundation. Bill cut logs while Ellen, Dad, and I built the foundation.

After we had finished the foundation, Ellen and I peeled the bark off the logs. The men helped us the first thing in the morning and the last thing at night.

One morning Bill flew to Fairbanks for supplies. Dad took his gun and left camp. He had seen bear tracks and thought he could get us some meat.

An hour later we heard a shot somewhere on the other side of the lake. Soon Dad came out of the woods and said he'd shot a bear. He and I untied the airplane dock and rowed it across the lake to get the bear.

It was a black bear. Dad acted as if he shot a bear every day.

"Your dad always was the best bear hunter in the North," Bill told me when he flew in with supplies.

We started putting up the cabin the next day. I was surprised that Dad knew how to do everything. He gave all the orders. And he was sure good with an ax.

"Best man in the West when it comes to using an ax," Bill told me.

The cabin went up fast. In a few days we had the walls done and were working on the roof. We cut out windows and a door.

At last the big cabin was really something to be proud of. It had big windows on the side that overlooked the lake. There were two big rooms downstairs and some bedrooms upstairs.

By then it was getting dark earlier. The air was cool, and some of the leaves had started to turn yellow and red. We knew it was time for us to go, but we didn't want to.

"Why don't you stay?" Bill asked. "We can run the business together."

Dad shook his head. "It sounds like fun," he said. "But we could only work part of the year. There's just enough business for the two of you. Besides the boy has to go to school. Maybe we can come back again."

Dad sold his car in Fairbanks, and he and I flew home in a jet. I hated to see him shave off his beard because without it he looked just like an ordinary man. But I knew that he was no ordinary man.

I guess lots of people may be like my dad. You think there's nothing special about them. Then you find out that they can do all kinds of things you didn't know about.

That summer in Alaska, I learned a lot about my dad. I learned that he was special.

Reflections

1. What was life like at home for Dad and his son?
2. Why do you think Dad decided to go to Alaska?
3. What did Dad say when his son told him that no one else knew what to do for the man with the broken leg?
4. How did Dad act after he shot the bear?
5. Why did Dad decide not to stay in Alaska?
6. What kinds of transportation were used in the story?
7. Write two or three sentences about the things you would do if you went to Alaska on a vacation.

DOES IT FIT?

Read the sentences below. Do they fit the pictures?

Kiya would sweep the sky.

The statue was in the heart of the city.

The bear charged.

Ann Marie was a city kid.

Which word in each sentence has more than one meaning? Do you know other words like that? Use them in sentences. Then draw funny pictures to go with them.

THE SWINGING BRIDGE

Millicent Humason Lee

It was early dawn in the mountains of Mexico. In an Indian village hidden in the evergreen trees, cold dawn was creeping into a tiny hut. Marcos turned over on his sleeping mat of woven palm. Cold dawn touched his shoulder. He turned over again. Cold dawn met his face. And then he remembered!

This was the day he was going to the great city to find work! This was the day he was going to leave his home.

Now the Indian boy got up stiffly. He moved his legs and arms until they felt easy again. The boy put on his jacket. Then he took his pointed hat from a hook and set it over his thick, black hair. He rolled his sleeping mat and rain cape into a snug bundle for his back.

Now Marcos was ready for the trail. He looked at his sleeping parents and stole out of the hut.

"I will not wake them," he said to himself. "They are tired out from planting the corn yesterday, and they know that I must take the trail at dawn."

Down, down, down the trail he went into the valley, and then up, up, up again. In the late afternoon, the mountainside he was climbing grew steeper and steeper.

He stopped on the mountaintop and looked down. Under his black hat, his dark eyes were wide. His chest rose and fell quickly under his dusty jacket. He was looking into a deep, wide canyon between this mountain and the mountain ahead. Steep, sharp rocks faced each mountain. Far down in the canyon between the mountains ran a river that looked like a thread of blue yarn.

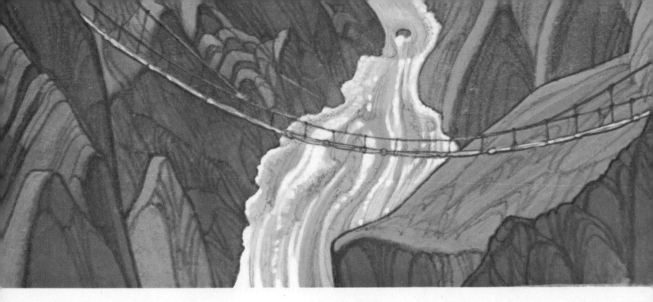

But that was not all. Hung from mountainside to mountainside was a swinging bridge made of vines. It looked as frail as a spider web as it hung there shimmering in the setting sun. In the middle it dipped way down.

How could Marcos have forgotten this swinging bridge? His mother and father had talked about it many times. But somehow it had seemed more like a dream bridge than a real bridge. And now he would have to cross it.

Slowly he wove his way down through the rocks to the swinging bridge of vines. Right across the canyon it hung, quiet now that no footsteps were upon it.

The boy remembered a story his father had told him one day. An old woman of the tribe was afraid to cross the bridge. One of the men used his red sash to blindfold her so that she could not see the water far below. Then she crossed easily. But one man walked before her and one behind.

Marcos closed his eyes. He could feel his heart beating. He could almost hear it beating. He looked back toward the trail over which he had come. Would he have to turn back?

"There is no one to blindfold me with his sash," he thought. "Shall I blindfold myself? That would not be wise, for there is no one to walk before me. No one." Marcos thought a long minute. "Shall I go back?" Then he laughed aloud and faced the bridge again.

"If this bridge holds others, it will hold me. How can I reach the great city unless I cross this bridge? It will always stand between me and the great city."

Now bravely he set one dusty foot on the bridge and took hold of the vine rail with one hand. The bridge swung like a spider web in the wind. He closed his eyes tight. Then he opened them wide again. He took one step, and then another, and then another. Soon he was walking in the very middle of the bridge.

He kept his eyes on the mountain before him. "I must not look down!" he thought. But it seemed as if he must look down. A voice in the river seemed to be calling, "Look down! Look down!"

And then Marcos laughed aloud again. **"You can't fool me, old river! I won't look down, but even if I did, you wouldn't make my head spin! This is the bridge of my people and I am at home on it!"**

And so Marcos crossed the bridge made of vines for the first time. And he felt a little ashamed that he had been afraid of such a beautiful thing.

"I have done the hardest thing first," he thought, as he walked up the other mountain. "Now things will not seem so hard in the great city."

Reflections

1. Why did Marcos leave for the city at dawn?
2. If you were Marcos, would you have crossed the swinging bridge? Why or why not?
3. Why did Marcos decide to cross the bridge?
4. What is the greatest problem you ever had to overcome? How did you solve it?
5. How did talking to himself give Marcos courage?
6. Pretend you are Marcos. Write what you think will happen to you on your first day in the city.

BRIDGES

Old London Bridge was very wide
With shops and houses on each side.
And Brooklyn Bridge is very high;
It seems to hang down from the sky.
But, oh, last night, from chair to table,
A spider flung her silver cable
And straight across the air she sped
Upon a bridge as thin as thread.

—Rowena Bennett

Charles Graves

Nellie Bly
Reporter for *The World*

A large newspaper in Pittsburgh first printed Nellie's byline. The year was 1885. A woman's name on a news story was news itself then. And Nellie was only eighteen when she first became a newspaper reporter.

Nellie grew up in a small town in Pennsylvania. She learned to read and write at a very early age. She liked books and had a good imagination. Soon she was writing stories to read to her friends.

When her family moved to Pittsburgh, Nellie went too. She knew that she must find work. "Why not get a job on a newspaper?" she thought.

But getting a reporter's job was not easy. Some people felt that only men should report the news. Before she was hired, Nellie had to write a special story. It was so well written that she got the job.

At first, Nellie wrote mostly about the city's workers and their jobs. Then she was asked to write about weddings, parties, clothes, and the like. These things did not interest her as much.

Later, Nellie moved to New York City. She wanted to write for *The World*. That paper, she knew, always fought for the rights of poor people. As a reporter for *The World,* Nellie could write about anything she wished.

In 1889, Nellie made a trip around the world for her paper. Out of this trip came the travel reports that made her famous. What you are about to read is the story of Nellie's trip.

The World

Nellie always liked books about travel. One of the best, she thought, was *Around the World in Eighty Days*. This was written, in 1872, by the Frenchman Jules Verne.

In Verne's book, the hero makes a bet for a great deal of money. He bets that he can go around the world in eighty days. At that time, few people made such a long trip. And those who did, found that it took them a year or more. There were no airplanes or cars then.

In the story, Verne's hero wins his bet. But most people who read the book thought such fast travel impossible. Nellie, though, believed she could make the trip in fewer than eighty days.

She tried to get her newspaper to pay for the trip. Nellie knew that it would cost a great deal of money. But she also thought *The World* would make even more money from it. Many people would buy *The World* just to read about her travels.

"The trip is a good idea," one of the men at *The World* finally said. "But a man should be the one to go."

"If you send a man," Nellie answered, "I'll start the same day for another paper. And I'll beat him, too."

The men who ran *The World* were afraid Nellie would do just that. So they let her go. She was to send back reports to the paper by telegraph. She was to tell *The World* about the world as she saw it.

On November 14, 1889, Nellie sailed for England from Jersey City. "I'm off," she said as the ship sailed away from the dock. "And I'll be back before the eighty days are up."

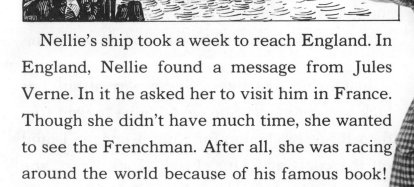

Nellie's ship took a week to reach England. In England, Nellie found a message from Jules Verne. In it he asked her to visit him in France. Though she didn't have much time, she wanted to see the Frenchman. After all, she was racing around the world because of his famous book!

Nellie stopped to see the Vernes on her way to Italy. "What a child," Mr. Verne said when he met her. "Can it be that a baby is going all that long way alone?"

Mrs. Verne turned to her husband. "Nellie is young and strong," she said. "I believe, Jules, that she will make the hero in your book look foolish. She will make the trip faster than he did."

Nellie smiled.

Jules Verne didn't speak English very well, but he tried. As Nellie got ready to go, he asked, "How does one say in English *'bonne chance'*? Good duck? Very well, good duck, Nellie."

Nellie laughed, but Verne didn't mind. "Oh, it's good luck, not good duck," he said. "Well, no matter, the feeling is the same in either case."

After leaving the Vernes, Nellie went by train through France into Italy. At a seaport in Italy she got on a ship. Her next stop was Ceylon, a large island off India. The trip, so far, was going well.

In Ceylon, however, Nellie was afraid her luck was changing. She would have to wait five days for a ship bound for Hong Kong, an island off the coast of China. From Hong Kong, she was to sail for America on December 28.

Nellie was worried. If she missed the ship for America, all would be over. Her trip around the world would then take more than eighty days.

Still, nothing could be done about it at that point. So Nellie had fun seeing the sights of the island. She went all over Ceylon in a little cart pulled by two men.

Near her hotel, Nellie saw a snake charmer with his little basket. He asked her if she would like to see a snake dance. Nellie gave him some money.

The man lifted the lid of the basket. Out came a deadly cobra. The snake charmer waved a red cloth at the snake. At the same time, he played some music.

The angry cobra rose up and struck at the cloth. As the man raised the cloth higher, the snake also rose higher. Finally, it was standing on its tail.

Nellie was frightened when the snake struck at the snake charmer. But the man was too quick for the cobra. He caught it by the head. Then he put it back in the basket.

Sightseeing was fun. But Nellie was glad when her ship finally sailed for Hong Kong. She hoped it would get there in a hurry. If it did, she would surely catch the ship for America.

Soon, however, Nellie began to worry. She sometimes even found it hard to sleep. The ship on which she was traveling seemed so slow.

On the way to Hong Kong, the ship stopped at a large port. In a pet shop, Nellie saw a small monkey and fell in love with it. "Will the monkey bite?" she asked the storekeeper.

"No," he answered. "This is a good monkey."

Nellie bought it. "I won't be alone anymore," she said.

After leaving the port, Nellie's ship picked up speed. She was excited when it reached Hong Kong on time. The ship for America was still there. "Now I'll surely circle the world in less than eighty days," she thought.

Bad news, though, was waiting for Nellie in Hong Kong. Another woman was also racing around the world. Her trip had started the day after Nellie left New York. She had headed West, rather than East as Nellie did. The woman's name was Elizabeth Bisland. And a newspaper was also paying for her trip.

Elizabeth Bisland had passed through Hong Kong going the other way some days before. She told everyone that she could travel faster than Nellie.

Nellie was almost sick with worry. What if Elizabeth Bisland reached New York before she did? Nellie tried not to think about it.

After a stop at Japan, the ship ran into a storm. At once, the captain cut down on the ship's speed. Some people thought Nellie's monkey brought bad luck. They even wanted to throw it overboard. Nellie hid her pet until the storm had passed.

She could not, however, stop worrying about the ship's speed. Would Elizabeth Bisland beat her around the world? Finally, Nellie went to see the ship's captain.

"I would rather return dead and on time than alive and late," she told him.

The captain promised to go faster. Signs on the ship's bulletin board read:

We'll Win or Die for Nellie Bly

After that, the ship put on speed. When it reached San Francisco, Nellie felt hopeful. Before leaving, she thanked the captain and crew.

With her monkey sitting on her arm, Nellie got on a special train. Now began the race across America to New York. All along the way, crowds came to see Nellie Bly.

On January 25, 1890, the train reached Jersey City. Nellie had left there seventy-two days, six hours, and eleven minutes earlier. Jules Verne's hero took almost eight days longer to circle the globe than she had. Elizabeth Bisland was still at sea somewhere off Europe. Nellie had won the race around the world!

A big crowd was waiting to meet her. Nellie stepped off the train. She threw her hat into the air with joy. The crowd roared. On the river each ship blew its whistle in her honor.

Nellie was taken across the river to New York by boat. Then she went to *The World* building. Crowds there shouted, "Nellie Bly!"

That day, Nellie's story covered *The World's* front page. Messages came from everywhere. The one she liked best was from Jules Verne.

Nellie didn't go right back to work for *The World*. She went on a speaking trip all over America. But first she gave her monkey to a zoo. She knew he would be happier there.

Nellie's speeches around the country made world travel better known. She told how safe and easy it was to go to faraway places.

But people learned more than that from Nellie's trip. Her writings showed them that women can do a fine reporting job. From that time on, women found the newspaper field more open to them. It was no longer surprising to find a woman's name on a byline — thanks to Nellie Bly.

Reflections

1. Why are there more newspaper reporters today who are women than in 1885?
2. What kinds of transportation did Nellie use during her trip around the world?
3. Why didn't Nellie go right back to work for *The World*?
4. Would you like to be a newspaper reporter? Why or why not?
5. List in order the places where Nellie went.

Government
It's Your Business

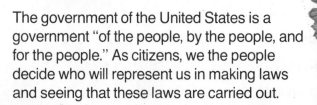

The government of the United States is a government "of the people, by the people, and for the people." As citizens, we the people decide who will represent us in making laws and seeing that these laws are carried out.

When you are old enough to vote, you will be able to take part in electing the people who will represent you. Perhaps, if you are qualified, you may be elected yourself!

But before then, you can start learning about our government. You can begin by finding out about the history of our country — how and why it was started. You can ask questions about the government of your own town or city and state. You can also get to know the people who represent you now and find out about the duties they perform.

As you learn, you will see that working to make our government even better is a way of serving others. It shows that you care about our country and its future. And it shows that you are proud to be a United States citizen.

Mr. Justice Thurgood Marshall has been an associate justice of the United States Supreme Court since 1967.

Ms. Azie Taylor Morton became Treasurer
of the United States in 1977.

Meeting and talking with people
is The Honorable Richard Lugar
who was elected a United States
Senator from Indiana in 1976.

Delivering a speech is The
Honorable Dixy Lee Ray, who
was elected Governor of the
State of Washington in 1976.

Sound of Sunshine, Sound of Rain

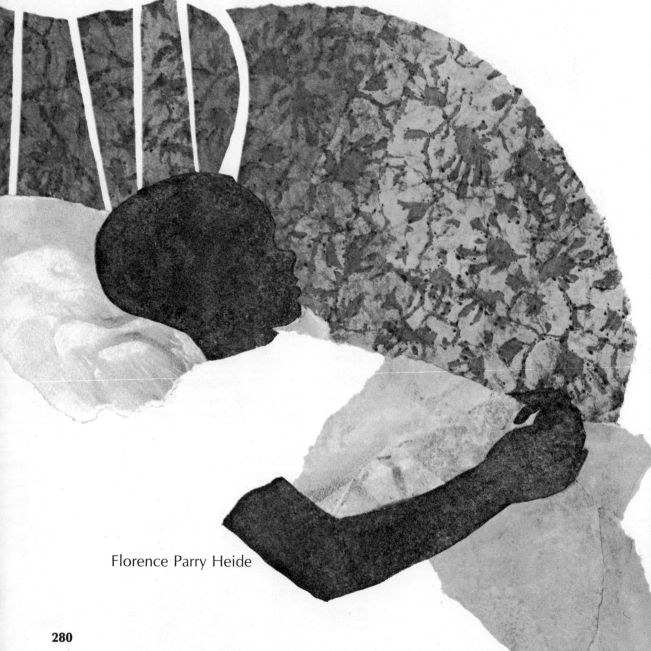

Florence Parry Heide

Part One

It must be morning, for I hear the morning voices.

I have been dreaming of a sound that whispers *Follow me, Follow me*, but not in words. I follow the sound up and up until I feel I am floating in the air.

Now I am awake, and I listen to the voices.

My mother's voice is as warm and soft as a pillow.

My sister's voice is little and sharp and high, like needles flying in the air.

I do not listen to the words but to the sound. Low, high, low, high, soft, hard, soft, hard, and then the sounds coming together at the same time and making a new sound. And with it all, the sharp sounds of my sister's heels putting holes in what I hear.

Then I hear the slamming of kitchen drawers and the banging of pans, and there is no more talking.

My bed is in the living room. I reach out to feel if my mother has put my clothes on the chair beside my bed. They are there, and I feel the smoothness and the roughness of them.

I reach under the chair to find which shoes my mother has put there. They are my outside shoes, not my slippers, so today must be a warm day. Maybe I can go to the park. I tap my good luck song on the wall beside my bed.

I put my feet on the floor and feel the cool wood. Then it is four steps to the table, then around the table, touching the chairs, and then seven steps to the window. I put my cheek against the window, and I can feel the warm sun. Now I am sure I can go to the park, if my sister has time to take me on her way to study.

I take my clothes into the bathroom, and I wash and dress there. Hot water, cold water, soapy water, plain water, loud water, still water. Then I make sure I have turned the faucets tight. I make sure I have buttoned all of my buttons the right way, or my sister will be cross, and maybe not have time to take me to the park.

I tap my good luck song against the door before I open it.

When I open the door, I hear the voices again. My sister's voice is like scissors cutting away at my mother's voice.

I sit at the table, and my mother gives me my breakfast. I breathe on the hot chocolate so I can feel it on my face coming back warm. I drink just a little at a time so I can keep holding the warm cup.

"*Eat while it's hot,*" says my sister to me loudly.

"Does he have to be so slow?" says my sister to my mother in her quiet voice. My sister thinks because I cannot see that maybe I cannot hear very well. She talks loudly to me, and softly when she does not want me to hear, but I hear.

"*Finish your hot chocolate,*" says my sister loudly.

"I can't be late," she says in her quiet voice to my mother. "Everybody's always late but me, and I won't be late."

After breakfast I go over to the window again. When I put my cheek against the glass, it is warmer than before, so today will be a good day. I tap my good luck song against the window.

My sister says she will take me to the park on her way to study. She tells me to wait for her outside on the steps.

I go down the outside steps. There are seven steps. Seven is my most magic number. Seven up, seven down, seven up, seven down. I go up and down, waiting for my sister.

My sister comes out. She takes my hand. She walks very fast, but I can still count the steps to the park, and I can still remember the turns. Someday I can go there by myself. I listen to the street noises and try to sort them out.

My sister's hand is not soft. I can feel her nails, little and sharp, like her voice, and I listen to her heels making holes in all the other sounds.

The park seems a long way off.

When we get to the park, we first go to the bench. She waits to make sure I remember my way in the park. Fourteen steps to the bubbler, around the bubbler, twenty steps to the curb.

I go back to the bench. I try to hurry so my sister won't have to wait long and be cross. Now seventeen steps to the telephone booth, four benches on the way, and I touch them all. Then I come back to the bench. My sister puts money in my pocket so I can telephone.

She talks to me and to herself.

"Filthy park," she says, and it is as if she were stepping on the words. "No grass. Trees in cages. Since when do benches and old newspapers make a park?"

Now she is gone, and I have my morning in the sun.

I try each bench, but mine is still the best one.

I go to the bubbler and press my mouth against the water and feel it on my tongue, soft

and warm. I put my finger on the place where the water comes out. I walk around and around the bubbler, and then I try to find my bench. It is one of my games. I have many games.

I walk over to the telephone booth, touching the four benches on the way. I stand inside the booth. I feel in my pocket to see if the money my sister gave me is still there. It is. I shall have enough left over to buy an ice cream bar after I telephone home.

I practice dialing our number so I will be sure I have it right. Then I put my dime in and call. I hear it ring two times. "Hello," my mother says. I tell my mother that I'm all right. "Take care," she says. We both say, "Good-bye."

I blow on the glass and it blows back to me. I tap my good luck song on it and go back to my bench.

I play one of my games. I listen to every sound and think if that sound would be able to do something to me, what it would do. Some sounds would scratch me, some would pinch me, some would push me. Some would carry me, some would crush me, and some would rock me.

I am sitting on my bench tapping my good luck song with my shoes when I hear the bells of an ice cream truck. I feel the money in my pocket. I still have a dime, and I also have a bigger coin. I knew I would have enough for an ice cream bar.

I walk out to the curb, touching the cages around the trees. I wait until the bells sound near, and I wave.

Part Two

The ice cream man stops. He is near enough for me to touch his cart. I hold out my money.

Now I feel him seeing me, but he does not take my money. "Here," I say, but he still does not take the money from me.

"Guess what?" he says, and his voice is kind and soft as fur. "Every tenth kid wins a free ice cream bar, and you're the lucky one today."

I can feel him getting off his cart and going around to open the place where he keeps his ice cream bars. I can feel him putting one near my hand, and I take it. I start back to my bench.

"You gonna be okay by yourself now?" the ice cream man calls, so I know he is seeing me.

I sit on the bench. I listen for the sound of his cart starting up, and his bells ringing. But I can only hear the other sounds, the regular ones. Then I hear him walking over to my bench.

I am sorry, because I only want to feel the ice cream and see how long I can make it last. I do not want anyone to sit with me, but he is sitting with me now.

He starts to talk, and his voice is soft as a sweater.

His name is Abram. He tells me about the park.

My sister says the trees are in cages because if they weren't in cages they wouldn't stay in such a terrible park. They'd just get up and go somewhere pretty.

Abram says the trees are in cages to keep them safe so they can grow up to be big and tall. "Like sides on a crib for a baby, keeping him from falling and hurting himself," says Abram.

My sister says the park is ugly and dirty.

Abram says there are a few little bits of paper, and a couple of cans and some bottles. But he says he can squint his eyes and all those things lying around shine like flowers. Abram says you see what you want to see.

My sister says the park is just for poor folks, and that no one would ever come if they had a chance to go anywhere else.

Abram says the park is just for lucky people, like him and me. He says the people who come to this park can see things inside themselves, instead of just what their eyes tell them.

After a while Abram goes away. He says he will come back and look for me tomorrow. I hear his ice cream bells go farther and farther away until I do not hear them anymore.

While I am waiting for my sister to come for me, I fall asleep on the bench.

I have a good dream. I dream that Abram lifts me so I can touch the leaves of a tree. All of the leaves are songs, and they fall around me and cover me. I am warm and soft under the songs.

My sister shakes me awake. "You'll catch cold lying here," she says.

The next day while I am sitting on my bench, I hear the ice cream bells. I walk out to the curb, touching the cages of the trees as I go. Abram gives me an ice cream bar and we walk together back to the bench. I do not have to touch the cages because I am with him.

After I finish my ice cream bar, Abram gives me some paper clips so I can feel them in my pocket. He shows me how I can twist them to make little shapes.

After he leaves, I feel them. There are seven paper clips.

That night I dream that someone is gathering in a big net everything in the world that makes a

sound, and I am tumbled in the net with dogs and cars and whistles and buses. I try to get out of the net and my sister shakes me awake.

"Stop thrashing around," she says. "You're all tangled up in the blanket."

The next day Abram brings me a balloon.

I can feel it round and tight. It tugs at the string.

Abram says some balloons are filled with something special that makes them want to fly away, up to the sun. This balloon is filled with that something special.

He says some people are filled with something special that makes them pull and tug, too, trying to get up and away from where they are.

His voice is like a kitten curled on my shoulder.

He tells me my balloon is red, and he tells me about colors.

He says colors are just like sounds. Some colors are loud, and some colors are soft, and some are big and some are little, and some are sharp and some are tender, just like sounds, just like music.

What is the best color, I wonder?

He says all colors are the same, as far as that goes.

There isn't a best color, says Abram. There isn't a good color or a bad color.

Colors are just on the outside. They aren't important at all. They're just covers for things like a blanket.

Color doesn't mean a thing, says Abram.

When my sister comes, she asks me where I got my balloon.

I tell her about my friend.

I hold on to the string while we walk.

When we get home, I tie the string of my balloon to my chair.

I have a bad dream in the night. I dream that my ears are pulling in every sound in the world, so many sounds I cannot breathe. I am choking with the sounds that are pulled into me and I have to keep coughing the sounds away as they come in, or I will smother.

"Here's some stuff for your cold," says my sister.

When I am awake again, I cannot tell if it is morning. I hear noises but they are not the morning noises. My sister has her quiet voice, and I do not hear the little hard sounds of her heels making holes in the morning.

She is wearing slippers. She tells my mother she is not going to go to study today.

There is no hurry about today. I reach for my balloon. The string lies on the chair, and I find the balloon on the floor, small and soft and limp. It does not float. It lies in my hand, tired and sad.

I lie there and listen to the sound of slippers on the kitchen floor.

I tap my good luck song against the wall over and over, but I hear the rain and I know I will not go to the park today.

Tomorrow will be a nice day. Tomorrow my sister and I will go to the park to find Abram. He will make my balloon as good as new.

I walk to the window and lean my head on it.

The rain taps its song to me against the glass, and I tap back.

Reflections

1. What clues show you that the boy is blind?
2. What senses are the most important to blind people? Why?
3. Why did the boy think it would be a good day?
4. Why did Abram sometimes squint his eyes?
5. How many days did the boy spend with Abram?
6. Pretend you are the boy. Close your eyes and listen to the sounds around you. Write what these sounds tell you about your world.

Voices

There are songs and sounds in stillness
In the quiet after dark,
Sounds within sounds,
Songs within songs.
There are rhythms in the quiet
And pulses in the night,
Beats within beats,
Drums within drums.

Something calling in the embers,
Something crying in the rocks,
And out beyond the darkness
There are voices in the stars.

—Felice Holman

298

Clare K. Galbraith

Angelina's Two Worlds

My name is Angelina, which means "Little Angel." Sometimes I don't feel like an angel. Sometimes I don't act like an angel, either.

Early last week, after school, my big brother Juan kept saying, "Come on, slow poke. Hurry up. Mama has *pan dulce* at home." He knows I like sweet rolls and hot chocolate after school. Most days I run and skip home, but that afternoon my feet seemed heavy. I didn't know how I felt.

In class that day, Miss Murray, my teacher, invited all our mothers to come to school. They were to come the next Tuesday, the second of March. Miss Murray gave me a note to give to Mamacita. The second of March is Texas Independence Day. Juan's class would give a play. Our class would show what we learned.

Right away, I began to worry. I hardly heard Miss Murray as she told us the story of Davy Crockett and the Alamo. Did I really want Mama to come to school to see what we do? Did I really want my teacher to meet my mother? I wasn't sure. My home and my school were so different. Juan felt the same way. He said it was like living in two worlds that were always apart.

As we walked along, I thought about what Juan had said. We do live in two worlds, I said to myself, one at home and one at school. At home we speak mostly Spanish. Uncle Pancho says that our house keeps him from ever being homesick for Mexico. It is filled with many interesting things that Mama and Papa brought from their old home. Mama is already teaching me how to cook the easiest Mexican dishes. (Juan knows how to cook a whole Mexican meal.) School always seems very far away when we are at home.

At school we speak English and do our lessons in English. Some of us in class speak Spanish better than we speak English. (Often we find it hard to change from thinking in one language to thinking in the other.)

Sometimes we feel that Miss Murray speaks too fast. Or we don't understand what she is saying. Then I look on Maria's paper, and Maria looks on Rosa's paper. We aren't copying. We are just trying to guess what Miss Murray means. Then we all giggle. Miss Murray doesn't know why we giggle. She thinks we are being bad. Maybe she thinks we are laughing at her.

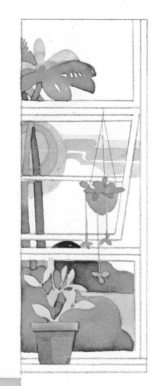

Suddenly, Juan's voice broke into my thoughts. "I know you're thinking about Miss Murray's note to Mama," he said. "But don't worry. Mama has never gone to our school. Why do you think she'd go now?"

By then, we were home. Mama was waiting, happy to see us. "Give her the note," Juan told me. I took it from my pocket and gave it to Mama. Mama looked at it, smiled, then put it in her apron pocket.

Mama says we go to school to learn. "When you grow up, who knows what you will be?" she often says. Then we daydream about it.

I see myself as so many things. Sometimes I'm in a ballet costume, dancing on a stage. Or I'm flying a jet airplane, taking people to Mexico. Or I'm an artist, painting beautiful pictures. Or I'm a secretary, writing important letters.

"Who knows?" says Mama, whenever we daydream. "But for now you must work hard at school. You must respect your teacher, and you must learn all you can."

"Are you coming to our school, Mama?" I asked that day as we were having our *pan dulce* and hot chocolate. Mama wrinkled up her eyes. "We'll see what Papa says when he comes home on Friday," she said. (Papa works for the government and is away for several days each week.)

When Mama smiled I suddenly forgot to worry. For a little while, I stopped thinking about the difference between my home and my school. Miss Murray will love Mama when she smiles, I thought. And I also thought, Mama will love Miss Murray. My teacher will let Mama see my notebook with my map of Texas. She will let her see all the papers that I wrote in school over the past week. On one of the big class maps, Mama will see where our families come from: some from Mexico, some from distant states, most from other places in Texas.

Then I began to wonder. If Mama came to my school, would she be proud of my work? I knew I had to let Miss Murray know that sometimes I didn't understand what we were to do in class.

In school the next day, I had an idea. If I didn't understand something I slipped up and whispered to Miss Murray. Then she came to show me. I began to do my very best work. It felt good to know how to do every lesson.

Then I noticed that Miss Murray went to help Maria and Rosa too. We did not have to guess what the teacher wanted us to do. We did not look at each other and giggle anymore. And none of the other children stopped their work to look at us.

On Friday nights when Papa comes home, I always wait for him out in front. This time, when he stopped his car, I jumped into his arms and kissed him hard.

He laughed. "What do you want now, my little angel?" But somehow I couldn't say.

After supper we all sat on the back porch. I sat next to Papa. I saw Mama wink at him. She patted her apron pocket.

Night came early. After my bath, I went to kiss them good night. They were talking. Papa rumpled my hair. He said quickly, "Good night, Angie." Mama hurried me off to bed. Sometimes she tells me a story or sings me to sleep . . . but not that night.

Saturday and Sunday went by slowly. After bedtime Sunday evening, I heard Uncle Pancho at the door. He called as he came in. Sleepily I heard his low voice with Mama's and Papa's. A few times I heard a laugh mix with the voices, then Papa asking, "Who's to say?" I was surprised to hear that they were speaking English, and not Spanish. I could not tell if Mama was talking to Papa and Uncle Pancho about Miss Murray's note.

"Mama, it's Monday," I said the next morning at breakfast. "Are you coming to school tomorrow?" She nodded. Papa had said yes, and Uncle Pancho would drive her.

That day Miss Murray went over all the past week's lessons in class. She came to each of us to ask if anything in the lessons gave us trouble. I found that now I was not afraid to speak out.

Today is Tuesday, the day the mothers were invited to our school. This morning, I kept looking out the window, oh, so many times. I almost missed my turn to read in reading group. I was wondering what Mama would wear. It might be her pink dress with the pink hat that she wears on Sundays, I thought. It could be the green suit that she wears to town with Papa.

After lunch we put all our papers on our desks. Maria and I put cups for punch on a table. Juan's class was ready for the play. I saw him with his costume on in the hall. He looked so brave. The play showed Mexican Texans fighting with Davy Crockett inside the Alamo.

"Ah," I said to myself, "here comes Mama and Uncle Pancho now." I was so happy I could hardly see anything . . . just sort of a golden light. Uncle Pancho was standing by the door. I was proud he was my uncle. Some of the other children were showing him their pictures. I went to Mama and put my hand in her hand.

Miss Murray said, "Buenos días, Señora Reyes!"

Mama smiled her lovely smile. I heard her say in English, "How do you do, Miss Murray? Angie is always talking about you. She is learning so much!" (To think I was worried about Mama coming to school!)

Then I heard Miss Murray say, "And I am learning so much from Angelina. . . . She has helped me to be a better teacher."

Can you imagine that? I felt so light I wanted to fly. Maybe this is the way a real angel feels.

309

Going home I told Mama about my two worlds that seemed so far apart . . . until today. Mama said she knew how I felt. "I wanted to feel closer to your school," she said. "So for some time now I've been taking a course in English. I go in the mornings. Papa knew, of course, but the other night I surprised Uncle Pancho. He and Papa think my English is much better already." And Mama laughed.

But that wasn't all. Mama will go on our next field trip. She will help with the children. Miss Murray asked her today while Mama was drinking punch and looking at our big class map.

Reflections

1. Would you like to live in "two worlds"? Why or why not?
2. How can speaking two languages help you?
3. Why is thinking in one language different from thinking in another language?
4. Why did Angelina start to do better school work?
5. Make a list of the Spanish names and words used in the story. Write the English name or meaning next to each word if you can.

Singing

The children are singing,
their mouths open like sleepy fish.
Our teacher conducting the class
waves her arms
like a rhyme in water.
The girls sing high:
our ears ring for the sweetness.
Listeners stand in dazzling amazement.

—Peter Shelton, age 10

The Wisest Man in the World

Benjamin Elkin

Part One

In days of old, so it is said, a little bee flew into the castle of the great King Solomon. The angry guards ran to trap it. But the bee got away from them and flew to the King for safety.

Now this King was the wisest man in the world—so wise that he could speak the language of every living thing.

"O King," said the bee. *"Spare me today that I may live to serve you tomorrow."*

King Solomon smiled to think that this tiny bee could ever hope to serve a mighty king. But he drew the curtains and gently let the bee go with his own hand.

"Go in peace," he said. "I want nothing in return."

Through the open curtains the King saw a great caravan. There were many animals wearing jewels and gold. And at the head of the caravan rode the proud and beautiful Queen of Sheba.

The Queen and her caravan had come far across the wide desert to visit the King.

The King, dressed in his royal robes, was seated on his throne. It was a magnificent throne. On each side of the six steps leading to the throne stood two golden lions and two golden eagles. These golden lions and eagles allowed no one to lie to the King. If anyone dared to tell a lie, the lions roared and the eagles screeched.

When the Queen of Sheba entered, she could not hide her surprise at King Solomon's magnificent throne.

"May the King live forever," she said. *"I come as a true friend."*

At once, the golden lions roared and the eagles screeched. For the Queen had told a lie. She did not come as a true friend. But she knew nothing of the lions and eagles. So she bowed politely, thinking this was a royal greeting.

The Queen of Sheba had been jealous of King Solomon for a long time. During her visit she was hoping to shame him before his own people and even before the whole world.

During the next few days the Queen of Sheba did her best to show that King Solomon was not really wise.

She asked him riddles, but he answered all of them.

She brought him a large jewel with a winding hole through it. Then she asked him to draw a thread through it.

King Solomon only smiled and sent for a silkworm. The worm crawled through the hole, drawing a silk thread through it.

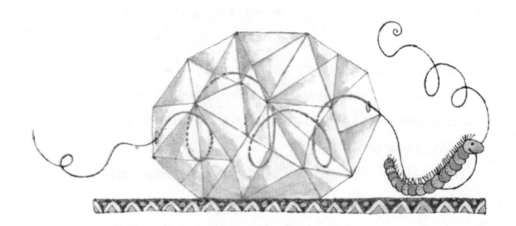

Another time, the Queen sent in sixty little boys and girls, all dressed alike. "If you please," she said, "tell me from your throne which are boys and which are girls."

The King sent for bowls of water to put before each child. Then he bid them wash their faces.

The boys splashed water on their faces while the girls dabbed the water with their fingertips. And so the King could easily tell them apart.

Once the King and Queen saw that a little dog had fallen into a deep pool. The water was so low that the dog could not be reached. King Solomon threw a log into the water for the dog to climb on.

"I would not have done so," said the Queen. "It is better to drown quickly than to die slowly of hunger." And she was happy, thinking that at last the King had done something that was not wise.

But King Solomon did not stop to answer. He showed his men how to block the nearby stream with rocks. As the stream spilled over into the pool, the water rose higher and higher. Soon the log floated up within reach, and the dog was safely lifted out.

Part Two

That night the Queen of Sheba met with her councilors. "So far we have had no success," she said, "and tomorrow will be our last chance. The King has invited people from many lands to a banquet in my honor. For this banquet we *must* find a trick that will show them that King Solomon is not wise, but a fool."

"Such a trick we have found," said the Queen's councilors.

From King Solomon's garden the councilors plucked a flower. Then they ordered their artists to make ninety-nine false flowers exactly like it. After this was done, the councilors placed just one fresh flower among the ninety-nine false ones. The Queen of Sheba herself could not point out the real one.

"Well done," said the Queen. "King Solomon will surely mistake a false flower for a fresh one from his own garden. By tonight he will be a joke among all his people."

One of the King's servants heard this and told the King. But King Solomon had become so proud and so sure of himself that he did not worry about it.

319

"It matters not," he said. "It suits me well that they should show how wise I am before all my people. I fear not what they may do."

That night the castle shined with lights as hundreds of people came to honor King Solomon and the Queen of Sheba.

At just the right time, the Queen said, "O King, my artists wish that you judge their work. Among these flowers only one comes from your garden. The others were made by my artists in your honor. Won't you pick out your own flower and let my artists know how real theirs look? Smell them. Touch them," she told the King.

At first the King was sure that he could find
the real one. But they all smelled the same. He
felt them, but they all felt the same. Maybe
this was a trick, and *all* the flowers were false.
Then he would be wrong no matter which one
he picked.

Never had King Solomon believed he could
be tricked. As he stood there, the people began
to whisper. "What is wrong? Can't the King
pick out a flower from his own garden? Maybe
he is not so wise after all!"

Then King Solomon felt something tickling his hand. A little bee had landed there. "I am here to help you," whispered the bee.

It flew low over the flowers. Then it crawled into the one flower that had honey inside.

No one else had seen the little bee. King Solomon leaned over and plucked the one flower with the bee in it, the one flower that had grown in his garden.

"Yes," said the King, "your artists do very fine work. But the false cannot be true. The others are false, and this one is true."

The Queen looked at the flower and saw that it was the single real flower.

Later in the quiet of his rooms, King Solomon thought of the little bee that had served him so well. He bowed his head. "I have been too proud," he said. "No one is so great that he needs no help. And no one is so small that he cannot give it."

Surely, wisdom is given
to all living things,
And the tiniest creatures
are teachers of kings.

Reflections

1. What special ability did the King have because he was so wise?
2. What did King Solomon do when the bee first offered to help him?
3. What did the Queen of Sheba hope to do during her visit with the King?
4. Why was the Queen happy when the King threw the log into the water for the dog?
5. Why did the Queen meet with her councilors?
6. Why didn't the King worry when one of his servants told him about the Queen's plan?
7. Pretend you are the King. Write how you would thank and reward the bee the next morning.

The Secret Language

Ursula Nordstrom

Sooner or later everyone has to go away from home for the first time. It happened to Victoria North when she was eight. She was very home-sick when she came to the Coburn School. She had not wanted to go to a boarding school. Then she met Martha, who taught her the secret language. It was exciting to have a roommate like Martha. Martha had a great imagination. She often thought of fun things to do. Victoria thought Martha was wonderful.

Martha taught Victoria the secret language the first day they met. "Ick-en-pick is for when something is silly," Martha said. "Or like when someone is trying to get in good with a teacher. And is trying to be very sweet. You know. Goody-goody stuff is ick-en-pick."

Victoria nodded.

"Ankendosh," Martha went on, "is for something mean. Some people around here are very ankendosh. Now, leebossa is when you like something. When something is just lovely. Or when something works out just right, it is leebossa. For anything very nice, you can say leeleeleeleebossa. But that's only for something really wonderful. Understand?"

"Are there any other words?" asked Victoria.

"No. But maybe we can make up some," Martha said.

"That would be leebossa," Victoria said. Martha smiled at her.

From then on Martha and Victoria were friends. Victoria was happier. But she still missed her mother. Victoria counted the days to winter vacation.

Slowly Victoria began to like some things about boarding school. But Martha didn't. Martha said every day that she was not coming back the next year. Victoria had to come back. And she wanted Martha to come back too.

The Halloween Costume Party

At breakfast the next day almost everyone was talking about the Halloween Costume Party.

"Do you know what you're going as?" Sue Burton asked Martha.

"Not yet," Martha said. "Vicky and I will go as something together. Won't we, Vicky?"

"What's it all about? What's it like, Sue?" Victoria asked.

"Oh, everyone comes in wonderful costumes. The people with the best ones get prizes. Last year I was a beautiful princess. Joe was a pirate. And Ann came as a witch."

"Vicky," Martha whispered, "we'll think of something different."

After breakfast Victoria asked about the party again.

"Oh, it isn't for two weeks," Martha said, "We have plenty of time."

A week later Victoria spoke about it once more. Martha told her not to worry.

"How about going as butterflies, Martha?"

Martha didn't answer.

The next day Victoria said, "How about going as ballet dancers?" Still Martha didn't answer.

Victoria was worried.

Finally it was only three days before the party. Martha said, "Well, I thought of something good."

"What, Martha?"

"Eyeglasses," Martha said.

"That's an awful idea," Victoria said.

"It's a leebossa idea, Vick. We'll make big round things out of paper. Then we'll draw a big eye on each of them."

"Martha Sherman! Why can't we go as something pretty?"

"Like some lovely butterflies?" Martha said.

"Oh Martha! Not eyeglasses!"

"All right," Martha said. "I'll think of something else."

Next she thought of chocolate ice-cream cones.

"They'll be easy to make," she told Victoria.

"Oh, Martha! That's not a good idea."

"I know where we can get some heavy cardboard for the cones. Then we'll get a lot of soft brown paper. We'll put the paper inside the cones so it will look like chocolate ice cream. It will be leebossa, Vick!"

"Couldn't we be flat-bottom cones?" Victoria asked. "Then we could at least have our legs out."

"Oh, Vicky! Anybody could do that. We have to be regular ice-cream cones."

"How will we walk?" Victoria asked.

"We'll leave enough room so just our feet can come out. It will be wonderful. We'll be two great big beautiful leebossa chocolate ice-cream cones."

Then Martha went to sleep. Victoria stayed awake for a long time. She was worried.

The next day they made the cones. But they couldn't find any soft brown paper.

"I know," Martha said suddenly. "Mrs. Coburn has soft green paper left over from her play. We can get some of that paper. Then we can go as pistachio ice-cream cones!"

"Oh, Martha!" cried Victoria. "That's a lee-bossa idea."

So they went as pistachio ice-cream cones. The space for their feet was so small they could hardly walk. And they could hardly see through the small openings. And of course they couldn't eat any of the food.

Finally it was time for the prizes. Sue Burton won the prize for the most beautiful costume. She wore an old-fashioned dress that belonged to her grandmother. Joe Bell won the prize for the best costume made by a student. He had come as Robin Hood. Then Mrs. Coburn said, "And now I'm sure we all know who should get the prize for The Most Original Costume. This prize should go to our two dear ice-cream cones."

Everyone clapped. Martha and Victoria
hopped slowly forward. Mrs. Coburn placed the
ribbon with "Most Original" on it in Victoria's
cone.

That night in bed Martha said happily, "It was
fun. Wasn't it, Vicky?"

"Yes," Victoria said.

"We'll start earlier next year," Martha
promised.

Victoria was happy that Martha had changed
her mind about coming back next year.

Then they both fell asleep.

Time seemed to pass quickly for Victoria after the party. Winter vacation was only a few days away. Victoria looked forward to seeing her mother again.

Soon Martha was able to sing:

"Three more days to vacation.
Then we go to the station.
Back to civilization.
Back to Mother and Home!"

During the bus ride to the railroad station Victoria and Martha hardly spoke. Finally Martha said, "No more days to vacation!"

The day that the vacation was over, Mrs. Coburn called all the girls together.

"Girls," Mrs. Coburn said, "I want you to meet your new housemother, Miss Denton."

A tall woman with soft gray hair stood up and smiled. "How do you do, girls?" she said. "I want to know you all well. I hope you will always come to me with any problems you have."

Victoria thought Miss Denton was lovely. Victoria noticed that Martha didn't look pleased.

Miss Denton went on, "I'll be very happy to have you call me Mother Carrie. I hope all of you will."

Victoria was surprised. You couldn't call a stranger that name! The girls left the room slowly.

Martha was waiting for Victoria in the hall. "The most ickenpick," said Martha.

Victoria nodded.

That night a bell instead of a whistle was used for lights-out. "A bell! How come?" wondered Martha.

Suddenly there was a tap at the door. The door opened. The new housemother must have heard them!

"Asleep, girls?" Miss Denton said softly.

There was no answer.

"Good," she said even more softly. She went to Martha's bed and tucked in her blankets. Then she tucked in Victoria, too.

"Sleep well," she whispered, and went out.

Both girls were silent after she left. "Maybe I wouldn't mind calling her Mother Carrie," thought Victoria. "She's nice." And she fell asleep.

Martha stayed awake a little longer. She thought the new housemother might not be so bad after all. Then she went to sleep, too.

The next morning the housemother came back to their room. She put her hand on Victoria's arm. "It's morning," she said softly. "Time to get up. Wake up. Breakfast in half an hour."

Victoria sat up in bed. She was surprised at being wakened so gently. "Why, hello, Miss Denton," she whispered.

The housemother went to Martha's bed and woke her in the same way.

"No whistle!" said Martha after the housemother left. "And no inspection! What do you think?"

"Pretty leebossa," Victoria said.

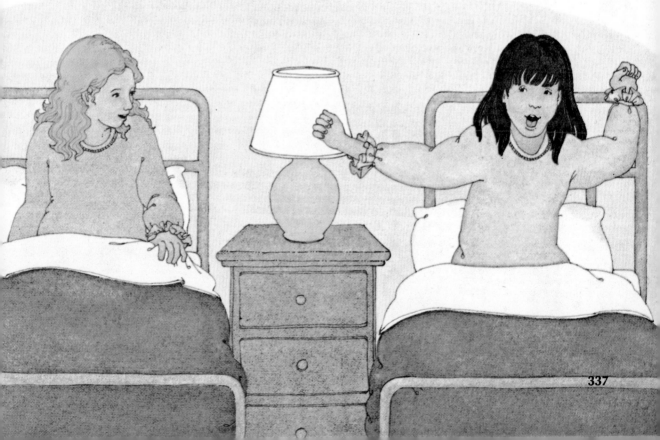

Within the next few days almost everyone liked Miss Denton. She never used a whistle. Every night she went into each room and told the girls good night. Every morning she woke them up. She really seemed to like children. When someone did something wrong she didn't yell. She would say, "Girls, that's not thoughtful." Or she would say, "Girls, that's not the right thing to do."

One afternoon there was a knock at their
door. It was Miss Denton.

"Girls," she said, sitting down. "I've been
thinking about this room. It is the smallest room
on this floor. It is very small for two girls."

Martha and Victoria looked at each other.
They hoped that they could still room together.

"I thought that we would take out the two
little iron beds and put in a double-decker bed.
How would you like that?" Miss Denton asked.

How would they like that! A double-decker
bed! On rainy afternoons they could really have
fun. They could hang blankets down from the
top bed and have a playhouse on the bottom one.
And after lights-out it would be much easier
to talk to each other. They couldn't believe it!

"We'd like it," Martha said. "Yes, we'd like
it very much."

"Fine. All the rooms will have them by next
year. But you may as well have yours now." She
smiled. "Goodbye, girls. I'll see you at supper."

"Martha, isn't she wonderful?"

"She seems all right. But I'm still not going
to call her Mother Carrie," said Martha.

Martha was always thinking of new fun things to do. For some time she had been thinking about having a midnight feast. She told Victoria, who also liked the idea. So they invited some of the other girls. On the night of the party Martha took ice cream, cake, cookies, candy, pickles, sardines, and orange drink out of her closet. Then she tried to keep Victoria awake. Finally she turned off her flashlight and lay down to wait for the others.

There was a loud noise. Martha woke up. It was morning! Miss Denton stood in the middle of the room. Her foot had hit the open can of orange drink. The ice cream had melted. Silently the housemother looked at the mess on the floor.

341

"Well, Martha," she said at last. "What is the meaning of this?"

"I just wanted to have a midnight feast," Martha said slowly.

"A midnight feast! You should not have done this, Martha. Did anyone else come, or was it just for you and Victoria?"

"We did ask others," Martha said. "But they didn't come. They went to sleep. Vicky went to sleep. And I guess I went to sleep too."

"Martha, what made you decide to have a midnight feast?"

"Oh, at boarding school you're supposed to have all these wonderful midnight feasts," Martha said. "So I thought we should have one."

"Oh, Martha." The housemother sighed. "You go out of your way not to do so many things you really are supposed to do."

Victoria was now awake. "I'm sorry," she said.

"You girls should not have done this. I am disappointed in you both. I'll talk to you later. But now you must clean up this mess. I'll get a mop." She shook her head and left.

That afternoon, after classes, Miss Denton called them to her room. "I've decided not to punish you this time. But I hope you learn a lesson from all of this. I don't know that you will."

"Thank you," Martha said.

"I want to talk to you girls about something I think of often. I like you two, as I like every child here. I think it is fine that you make up your own minds. The world will always need those who do not try to be just like everyone else."

She stopped and looked at them. Then she went on. "But you can't do exactly what you want all the time. You have to learn to act somewhere in between." She stopped and sighed. She didn't think they really knew what she was trying to tell them. "You may go now," she finally said.

Outside in the hall, Martha said, "Pretty ick-en-pick."

"I think she's pretty leebossa," Victoria said. They never talked about the feast again.

Soon it was spring vacation. After the vacation, the lovely spring days grew longer. On sunny days Miss Denton let the girls stay outdoors until seven-thirty. It was a beautiful time of the year.

Victoria loved Miss Denton. And by that time Martha loved the housemother too. They called her Mother Carrie now. Victoria had told Martha that it was leeleeleeleebossa to call the housemother Mother Carrie. Martha had said that it was all right. But Victoria knew better.

As the end of the school year grew closer, the days passed even more quickly. Soon autograph books were passed around. Everyone talked about final exams and summer vacation.

The days just flew by. Martha and Victoria passed all their exams. A few days later the children's trunks were brought to their rooms. The trunks had to be packed and sent home before the end of school.

Mother Carrie went from room to room to help the children pack. She found Victoria sitting inside her large trunk. "Well, girls," she said. "Glad to be going home at last?"

"Yes," said Martha.

"We'll miss you," said Victoria.

"Thank you, Victoria. I'll miss you girls, too. You've both grown up quite a bit this year. Do you feel you have?" the housemother said.

"I guess so," Martha said.

"What things have you learned this year? I don't mean just in school work."

"I learned how to make a bed," Victoria said.

"Anything else?"

"I learned the secret language," Victoria said.

"I wonder if you know that I've never liked your secret language," the housemother said. "I never told you because I suppose it is all right for children your age to have secrets. You'll learn, I hope, that it is not thoughtful to say things others cannot understand."

"If others don't like it, they can make up their own secret language," Martha said.

"None of the other children did that this year," Mother Carrie said. "If they had, I am sure you would not have liked it."

Martha smiled. "I learned that a midnight feast is no fun," she said.

"I learned not to be homesick," Victoria said.

"I think you both learned a great deal. But we won't talk about it any more now. I'll come back later to help you pack."

Martha sat down on her bed. "You know what? I wanted to tell her I learned some housemothers are nicer than others."

"She's really nice," said Victoria.

"Yes, she sure is," said Martha.

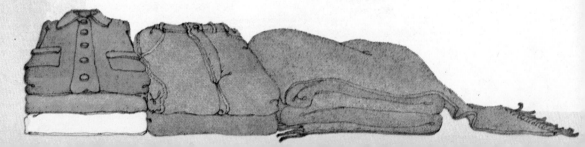

That night in bed Victoria whispered first. "Martha, are you coming back next year?"

"I don't know. I just don't know, Vicky. But I might have to come anyway."

"I'll have to come back. If you come back too, we could have fun, Martha."

"Maybe I will come back. If I do, we'll room together again. All right?"

"Oh, yes," whispered Victoria.

Then they both fell asleep.

On the last day of school, some children left in the morning. And others left in the afternoon.

Martha left in the morning. Victoria waved goodbye and then went back to their room. The empty room looked strange. She went downstairs and met Mother Carrie.

"Are you excited?" the housemother asked.

"Yes."

"I know you and your mother will have a lovely summer. And we'll see each other in the fall, won't we?"

"Yes," Victoria said. "Oh, I hope Martha will come back!"

"Maybe she will," Mother Carrie said.

"But it will be awful if she doesn't!"

"Even if she doesn't, you'll be all right," Mother Carrie said. "Remember, next year you'll be one of the old girls."

"Yes, I will be, won't I!" The thought surprised and pleased Victoria.

"Let's go to the dining room, shall we?" said Mother Carrie.

Later in the afternoon, Victoria and some of the other children waited for the bus. Mother Carrie and Mrs. Coburn came out to see them off.

"Now, here's the bus," Mother Carrie said. "Goodbye!"

"Goodbye, Mother Carrie!"

"Goodbye!" said Mrs. Coburn.

"Goodbye, Mrs. Coburn!"

Victoria sat at the back of the bus so she could look out the back window. Soon the buildings and the people became smaller and smaller. Finally the school was hidden by the green trees and the hills.

Reflections

1. In what year do you think this story takes place? Why?
2. Is Martha the kind of friend you would like to have? Why or why not?
3. What was the main reason Victoria and Martha didn't eat at the costume party?
4. Why did everyone like Miss Denton?
5. How did Victoria and Martha feel about getting a double-decker bed? Would you like to sleep in one? Why or why not?
6. Why did Martha want to have a midnight feast?
7. Pretend you are planning your favorite kind of party. Write two or three sentences about the food and special activities you would like to have.

Glossary

This glossary gives the pronunciations and meanings of some of the words used in this book.

The pronunciation is shown just after the word in this way: a·ble (ā′bəl). The letters and signs are pronounced as shown in the words listed below.

If the word has more than one syllable, as in the example, a heavy accent mark ′ is placed after the syllable that receives the heaviest stress.

PRONUNCIATION KEY

a	hat	i	it	ou	out	v	very
ā	face	ī	ice	p	paper	w	will
ä	father	j	jam	r	run	y	yes
b	bad	k	kind	s	say	z	zoo
ch	child	l	land	sh	she	zh	treasure
d	did	m	me	t	tell		
e	let	n	no	th	thin	ə	stands for
ē	be	ng	long	Ꝯн	then		a in about
ėr	her	o	hot	u	cut		e in given
f	fat	ō	open	u̇	pull		i in family
g	go	ô	or	ü	June		o in button
h	he	oi	oil				u in walrus

The pronunciation key, syllable breaks, and phonetic respellings in this glossary are adapted from the eighth edition of the *Thorndike-Barnhart Beginning Dictionary*. Users of previous editions or other dictionaries will find other symbols for some words.

FROM *THORNDIKE BARNHART BEGINNING DICTIONARY* BY E. L. THORNDIKE AND CLARENCE L. BARNHART. COPYRIGHT © 1974 BY SCOTT, FORESMAN AND COMPANY. REPRINTED BY PERMISSION.

A

ac·ro·bat (ak' rə bat) someone who can walk on tightropes, swing on trapezes, and do other such acts

Af·ri·ca (af' rə kə) one of the seven continents of the world

Al·a·mo (al' ə mō) a fort in Texas

A·las·ka (ə las' kə)

am·bas·sa·dor (am bas' ə dər) someone sent by one government to another to represent it

An·der·sen (an' dər sən), Hans Christian (hanz kris' chən)

An·gel (ān' jəl)

An·ge·li·na (an' jə lē' nə)

a·re·na (ə rē' nə) space in which contests or shows take place

ar·gyle (är' gīl) a knitting pattern of various colored diamond shapes; a sock knit in such a pattern

ar·row (ar' ō) a slender stick with a pointed head, which is shot from a bow

a·shore (ə shôr') on the shore; on land

A·tu (ä' tü)

B

back·stage (bak' stāj') behind the stage

badg·er (baj' ər) a grayfurred animal that lives underground

bal·let (bal' ā) a dance that usually tells a story

ban·quet (bang' kwit) a big feast

beam (bēm) a ray of light

blind·fold (blīnd' fōld') 1. to cover the eyes with a piece of cloth. 2. a covering for the eyes

board·ing school (bôrd' ing skül) a school with buildings where the pupils live during the school term

booth (büth) 1. at a fair, a small room in which goods are shown or sold. 2. a small closed room for a telephone or some other device

Bou·di·ni (bü dē' nē)

bra·vo (brä' vō) wonderful; well done

bub·bler (bub' lər) a drinking-water fountain

bull·doz·er (bùl' dō' zər) a powerful tractor used to clear land and move earth for buildings and roads

---

hat, fāce, fäther, let, bē, hèr, it, īce, hot, ōpen, ôr, oil, out, cut, pùll, Jüne, thin, ŦHen; ə stands for a in about, e in given, i in family, o in button, u in walrus.

bush·land (bush′ land) the wilds; a forest

Bush·men (bush′ mən) hunters that once lived in the bushland of South Africa

busi·ness (biz′ nis) **1.** work; a way of making a living. **2.** money made from selling goods or services: *In the summer Ben's hot dog stand does a good business.* **3.** a matter of interest: *We talked about class business.*

C

Can·a·da (kan′ ə də) the country lying on the northern border of the United States

can·yon (kan′ yən) a deep valley between steep mountainsides

cape (kāp) a coat without sleeves worn around the shoulders

car·a·van (kar′ ə van) a long line of people, animals, and wagons traveling together for safety across desert or wild country and often carrying goods to sell

cel·e·bra·tion (sel′ ə bra′ shən) special activities in honor of a special person, act, time, or day

Cey·lon (si lon′) a country that is an island in the Indian Ocean (now called Sri Lanka)

Christ·mas (kris′ məs) December 25, the holy day celebrating the birth of Jesus Christ

co·bra (kō′ brə) a deadly snake of Asia and Africa

colo·nel (kėr′ nl) an army officer

Co·pen·ha·gen (kō′ pən hā′ gən) the capital city of Denmark

cos·tume (kos′ tüm) **1.** style of dress, outer clothing. **2.** dress belonging to another time or place, worn on the stage or at masquerade parties: *The actors wore colonial costumes.*

coun·ci·lor (koun′ sə lər) a person who is asked for advice and gives advice

court (kôrt) the place where a ruler lives; royal palace

cray·fish (krā′ fish′) a shellfish that looks like a small lobster

croc·o·dile

(krok′ ə dīl) a large lizard that lives in warm waters and has a thick skin, powerful jaws, and a long body and tail

curb (kėrb) the raised edge of the pavement or sidewalk

D

de·cide (di sīd′) **1.** settle a question. **2.** give judgment. **3.** resolve; make up one's mind: *Mary decided to go to the party.*

De·li·lah (di lī′ lə)

de·sign (di zīn′) a pattern; a plan

di·al (dī′ əl) to turn the part of a telephone used in making calls

din·ing room (dīn′ ing rüm) a room where dinner and other meals are served

di·rec·tion (də rek′ shən) **1.** the way taken by something moving. **2.** telling what to do, how to do, or where to go; instruction

dock (dok) a large float or pier to which boats or seaplanes may be tied

dou·ble-deck·er (dub′ əl dek ər) two single beds one above the other

duck (duk) **1.** a swimming bird with a flat bill, short neck, short legs, and webbed feet. **2.** to lower or bend the body quickly to keep from being hit or seen.

dune (dün) a mound of sand

E

ea·gle (ē′ gəl) a large, powerful bird

en·er·gy (en′ ər jē) power or ability to work

em·per·or (em′ pər ər) in some countries, the name of the ruler

ev·er·green (ev′ ər grēn′) trees or bushes that stay green all year

F

Fair·banks (fer′ bangks) a city in the state of Alaska

fame (fām) being very well known

fau·cet (fô′ sit) water tap; spigot

fa·vor (fā′ vər) an act of kindness

fel·low (fel′ ō) a friend; a companion

filth·y (fil′ thē) very dirty

fin·ger·print (fing′gər print′) the marking of a fingertip on something: *The thief left his fingerprints all over the desk.*

flight (flīt) act of running away

foun·da·tion (foun dā′ shən) the part on which everything else rests

frail (frāl) weak; not strong

France (frans) a country in western Europe

G

Gha·na (gä′ nə) a country in Africa

glide (glīd) move smoothly, with grace and ease

gov·ern·ment (guv′ ərn mənt) people and groups that make and carry out the laws of a country

Gri·mal·di (gri mäl′ dē), **Jo·seph** (jō′ zəf)

gro·cer·y (grō′ sər ē) store that sells food and supplies for the home

---

hat, fāce, fäther, let, bē, hėr, it, īce, hot, ōpen, ôr, oil, out, cut, pùll, Jüne, thin, ŦHen; ə stands for *a* in about, *e* in given, *i* in family, *o* in button, *u* in walrus.

H

hand·cuffs
(hand′ kufs′) iron bracelets or rings that may be locked around the wrists to keep someone from using the hands

har·bor (här′ bər) a place where boats may dock

hare (her *or* har) an animal that looks like a rabbit but is much larger

haunt (hônt) visit often

herd (hėrd) **1.** a large band or group of animals. **2.** form into a flock or group

high·land (hī′ lənd) country or region that is higher and hillier than the neighboring country

Hong Kong (hong′ kong′) British colony on the coast of China

hon·or·ar·y (on′ ə rer′ ē) given or done as an honor or because one is thought highly of

Hou·din·i (hü dē′ nē), Har·ry (har′ē)

house·moth·er (hous′ muŦH ər) a woman who directs and takes care of a group of young people or children living together like a family in a house or building

house·wares (hous′ werz) small articles for sale for use in the house

I

i·mag·ine (i maj′ ən) form a picture in the mind; have an idea

im·pos·si·ble (im pos′ ə bəl) that cannot be or happen: *It is impossible for two and two to make six.*

In·di·a (in′ dē ə) a country in southern Asia

It·a·ly (it′ l ē) a country in the southern part of Europe

J

jew·el·ry (jü′ əl rē) jewels; objects worn on fingers, arms, around the neck, in the hair, or on clothes

join (join) come together with

K

Kath·a·rine (kath′ ə rin)
Ki·ya (kē′ yə)

L

lob·by (lob′ ē) a hall leading to the main room or rooms of a building, especially of a theater, museum, or hotel: *We met in the museum lobby.*

loom (lüm) machine for weaving threads into cloth

low·land (lō′ lənd) land that is lower and flatter than the neighboring country

Lyle   (līl)

M

Mac·Doug·al   (mak düg′ əl)

mag·i·cal   (maj′ ə kəl)   done by magic or as if by magic

ma·gi·cian   (mə jish′ ən)   one who does magic; a skilled performer of tricks

mag·nif·i·cent   (mag nif′ ə sent) richly colored or decorated; grand; splendid

main·land   (mān′ land′)   a large body of land that is not an island but lies off an island or islands

make·up   (māk′ up′)   paints, powder, and dress used by actors to play their parts

Mar·cos   (mär′ kəs)

Mex·i·co   (mek′ sə kō)   the country just south of the United States

mid·air   (mid′ er′)   the air above the ground

mid·get   (mij′ it)   **1.** very small. **2.** one who is very small

min·is·ter   (min′ ə stər)   in some countries, the director of a branch of government

Mit·zi   (mit′ sē)

moc·ca·sin   (mok′ ə sən)   a soft shoe, often made of deerskin and worn by Indians of North America

mod·el   (mod′ l)   a small copy

mo·tor·cy·cle (mō′ tər sī′ kəl) a bi-cycle run by a motor

mys·ter·i·ous·ly   (mi stir′ ē əs lē) without being seen or understood: *The eagle had returned just as mysteriously as it had disappeared.*

N

na·tion·al   (nash′ ə nəl)   belonging to a nation: *Thanksgiving is a national holiday in the United States.*

na·ture   (nā′ chər)   all things in our surroundings except those made by people

Nav·a·ho   (nav′ ə hō)   a tribe of North American Indians

neigh·bor·hood   (nā′ bər hůd)   **1.** a place where people live or work near one another. **2.** the people living or working in a place

O

O·den·se   (ō′ den sə)   a city in Denmark

of·fice   (ô′ fis)   a job or position, especially in government

or·di·nar·y   (ôrd′ n er′ ē)   not special

orig·i·nal   (ə rij′ ə nəl)   **1.** first; earliest. **2.** new; fresh: *It is hard to plan original games for a party.*

---

hat, fāce, fäther, let, bē, hėr, it, īce, hot, ōpen, ôr, oil, out, cut, půll, Jüne, thin, ᴛHen; ə stands for *a* in about, *e* in given, *i* in family, *o* in button, *u* in walrus.

ox·y·gen (ok' sə jən) one of the gases that make up the air and without which plants and animals cannot live

P

palm (päm) **1.** the inside of the hand between the fingers and the wrist. **2.** a palm tree and/or leaf tree that grows in warm places

Pan·cho (pän' chō)

Penn·syl·van·ia (pen' səl vā' nyə)

perch (pėrch) **1.** anything on which a bird can rest. **2.** to rest as birds do

per·form·er (pər fôr' mər) an actor; a player

pis·ta·chio (pis tash' ē ō) **1.** a greenish nut having a flavor that suggests almond. **2.** its flavor. **3.** light green

Pitts·burgh (pits' bėrg') a city in the state of Pennsylvania

plain (plān) **1.** clear; easy to understand. **2.** a flat piece of land

plas·tic (plas' tik) made of a synthetic material that can be molded

print (print) mark made by stamping or pressing on something with the foot or fingertip; track left by an animal

pro·ces·sion (prə sesh' ən) a parade

pup·pet (pup' it) a doll moved by wires or strings from behind or above a stage

R

raft·er (raf' tər) one of the beams that holds up a roof

re·hearse (ri hėrs') to practice

re·spect (ri spekt') honor; think highly of

rid·dle (rid' l) puzzling question

roam (rōm) go about with no special plan; wander

room·mate (rüm' māt) a person who shares a room with another

S

San Fran·cis·co (san frən sis' kō) a city in the state of California

scis·sors (siz' ərz) tool for cutting

Scot·land (skot' lənd) a part of Great Britain

screech (skrēch) cry out sharply in a high voice

sea·weed (sē' wēd') plants that grow in the sea

se·ñor·a (sā nyôr' ä) woman; Mrs.

shack (shak) roughly built hut

shears (shirz) **1.** large scissors. **2.** any cutting instrument resembling scissors; *grass shears*

She·ba (shē′ bə) in olden times, a kingdom in Arabia

sheep·herd·er (shēp hėr dər) a person who watches and tends large numbers of sheep on unfenced land

Si·bo·ni (si bō′ nē)

silk·worm (silk′ wėrm′) a caterpillar that spins a silk cocoon, or case, to lie in while it turns into a moth

sin·gle (sing′ gel) one

skunk (skungk) a black and white striped animal that gives off a strong smell when afraid or in danger

smoth·er (smuŦH′ ər) **1.** to not be able to breathe. **2.** to make unable to breathe

snail (snāl) small, slow-moving animal with a soft body protected by a shell

snug (snug) warm; comfortable

Sol·o·mon (sol′ ə mən) king of ancient Israel, famous for his wise acts

som·er·sault (sum′ ər sôlt) roll or jump, turning the heels over the head

sou·ve·nir (sü′ və nir′) something given or kept to remember a person, place, or happening

space·ship (spās′ ship′) an aircraft powered by rockets that can send it into outer space

spi·der web (spī′ dər web) a net spun by a spider in order to trap insects

splint (splint) a piece of wood used to hold a broken bone in place

spot·light (spot′ līt′) a lamp used to throw a bright light on a stage

squint (skwint) to partly close the eyes

stilts (stilts) two poles with steps for the feet

sup·plies (sə plīz′) things needed

sus·pense (sə spens′) feeling anxious, uncertain

T

tape re·cord·er (tāp ri kôr′ dər) a machine that makes a copy of sounds on plastic ribbon or tape

tat·too (ta tü′) mark with a pattern

tel·e·graph (tel′ ə graf) a way to send a coded message over wires by electricity

---

hat, fāce, fäther, let, bē, hėr, it, īce, hot, ōpen, ôr, oil, out, cut, pu̇ll, Jüne, thin, ŦHen; ə stands for a in about, e in given, i in family, o in button, u in walrus.

Tex·as (tek′ səs)

the·a·ter (thē′ ə tər) place where plays are put on or where movies are shown

thirst (thėrst) a strong desire for something to drink

thrash (thrash) move about; tossing and turning

thumb (thum) to go through: *I thumbed through the book.*

tight·rope (tīt′ rōp′) a tightly stretched rope or wire on which acrobats perform

tor·toise (tôr′ təs) a land turtle

trad·ing post (trā′ ding pōst) in the wilderness, a trading station or store where settlers or trappers may get supplies in return for furs or other goods

tra·peze (trə pēz′) a high swing on which acrobats perform

tuck (tuk) **1.** thrust into some narrow place. **2.** thrust the edge or end of a garment or covering closely into place: *Tuck your shirt in.* **3.** cover snugly: *Tuck the children into bed.*

tusks (tusks) long, pointed teeth: *Elephants and walruses have tusks.*

U

up·roar (up′ rôr′) a loud noise; excitement; a noisy disturbance

U·tah (yü′ tô)

V

va·ca·tion (vā kā′ shən) a holiday; time off from work or school

Verne (vėrn), **Jules** (jülz)

Vic·to·ri·a (vik tôr′ ē ə)

vine (vīn) a plant whose stem grows along the ground or up a wall or fence

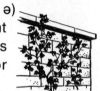

vol·ley·ball (vol′ ē bôl′) a game in which a ball is hit by hand back and forth across a net without letting it touch the ground

W

wa·ter hole (wô′ tər hōl) a natural hollow in the earth in which there is water

weath·er (weŦH′ ər) wear away by the sun, wind, and rain

weave (wēv) to make cloth out of thread

webbed (webd) **1.** like a spider web. **2.** having toes joined by a skin: *Ducks have webbed feet.*

wool (wul) **1.** the soft curly hair or fur of sheep and some other animals. **2.** yarn, cloth, or garments made of wool

wrin·kle (ring′ kəl) **1.** ridge; fold: *I must press out the wrinkles in this shirt.* **2.** make folds in: *Mama wrinkled up her nose.*